THE PERFECT
ENGLISH COUNTRY HOUSE

THE PERFECT
ENGLISH COUNTRY HOUSE

Candida Lycett Green

Photographs by Christopher Simon Sykes

RIZZOLI
NEW YORK

FOR RUPERT

AUTHOR'S NOTE

Houses are listed as being in the counties to which they have always belonged. The nearest large village or town is given to avoid any confusion. Please remember that *none of these houses is open to the public* except for Sandford Orcas Manor (p.14), Iford Manor (p.68) and Ebberston (p.82) which open on a seasonal basis. Trerice (p.18) is owned by the National Trust and is open to the public; other houses in this book belonging to the National Trust – Wilderhope Manor (p.23), Lodge Park (p.43) and The Old Parsonage (p.63) – can be viewed by special arrangement.

First published in the United States of America in 1991 by
Rizzoli International Publications, Inc.
300 Park Avenue South, New York, NY 10010

Published in Great Britain in 1991 by
Pavilion Books Limited

ISBN 0-8478-1373-8
LC 90-27561

Designed by Andrew Barron and Collis Clements Associates

Printed and bound in Italy

First printing

Frontispiece: The Lake House, Gloucestershire (see p. 100)

CONTENTS

INTRODUCTION
6

TUDOR TO EARLY RENAISSANCE
9

RENAISSANCE TO BAROQUE
39

GEORGIAN
81

REGENCY
117

VICTORIAN
135

EDWARDIAN TO THIRTIES
151

BIBLIOGRAPHY
172

INDEX
174

ACKNOWLEDGEMENTS
176

INTRODUCTION

This book is meant to be a layman's guide to the evolution of the smaller English house. I have chosen as perfect an example as I could muster of each stage of that evolution, but it is inevitably a personal choice rather than a text-book one. The smaller English house does not steer a straight and obvious course of architectural style, but veers off into strange and pleasurable directions like that of 'Strawberry Hill' Gothic or Victorian 'Queen Anne'.

The thread I have chosen to follow is that of houses I consider to be perfect period pieces or exceptional architectural masterpieces, and hence they are not always conventionally representative of their particular period. I may also have dwelt too long on the years between 1690 and 1730, but this was simply because it seems to be most people's favourite period. I asked innumerable friends and acquaintances which was their favourite house in England; almost invariably their choice was built between these dates. Three different people chose Mothecombe in Devon (1710), not least for its idyllic situation.

This is not the book of a scholar, as you will soon realize, but that of a genuine enthusiast. I derive untold pleasure from looking at buildings, but not just as objects which please the eye, nor just as works of art, as you would look at pictures in a gallery; I also like imagining who commissioned them, who built them, what sort of person first lingered on their balcony or opened their casement window. This book is an effort to pass that pleasure on.

The size of house chosen is meant to kindle a perfectly plausible dream. It should be possible to live in any one of them without staff, though some might need a large and willing family to maintain them. Over the doorway of a fine Georgian house called Knockhill in Scotland, there is the following line carved in stone: 'Too Small for Envy, for Contempt too Great'. This aptly describes the houses in this book, which were built on the whole by country gentry, tradesmen and clergymen, on a moderate scale, rather than by the aristocracy, who liked to flaunt their aesthetic views and show how cultivated they were on a much larger one.

Finding the perfect English house was easier said than done. At the outset, my criterion was that each house should be unadulterated and purely of its time. It was easy enough to find Victorian and Edwardian houses which had not been changed a jot, but with houses of earlier periods it became increasingly difficult. Frequently a Georgian house which I had always seen from the road and considered to be all of one date, was revealed, when I came to knock on its door, to be purely a façade built on to a much earlier building. Hence it is sometimes only the face in the photograph which represents the demonstrable and technical perfection, as at Netherhampton in Wiltshire, for instance. But despite the varying dates behind Netherhampton's front, the latter still ranks as a 'perfect' house to me.

Early houses which remain completely

untouched are few and far between, but a general rule emerged during my research for the book: the less important the house and the more remote its situation, the more old-fashioned it remained, like Hareston in Devon, which had no fashion-conscious owners wanting to show-off their taste and wealth to passers-by. Also, demotion from primary residence to tenanted farmhouse for a century or two, saved many a small grand house from a buffeting by the winds of changing style, as at Croan in Cornwall, Beckley in Oxfordshire or Mothecombe in Devon.

The pattern of change of many of the houses built before 1700, and the fluctuating fortunes of their owners provide a pretty good history lesson. When Henry VIII severed his relationship with the Church of Rome, many of the Italian craftsmen who were in England went home or to Ireland. Our classical development was hence later than in some other European countries.

Old land-owning families prospered and built under Queen Elizabeth I's reign, but many of them became badly unstuck during the Civil War. Nearly every house in the book built before 1650 was owned by an active Cavalier, whose fortunes dwindled in consequence, and only one by a Roundhead, the builder of Lodge Park in Gloucestershire. After Cromwell, new squires, successful tradesmen, farmers and impoverished Cavaliers who had made good marriages then began to build new houses. If you look through a family history and hit upon an advantageous marriage, the chances are that you will find a new house or a completely restored one at around the same date.

The eighteenth century was a fairly settled time for the small English house, and saw the birth of the professional architect and the introduction of pattern books. The early 1800s produced a wealth of eccentric houses and *cottages ornées* by the seaside, built by the frustrated rich who were unable to go abroad during the Napoleonic Wars. By the time of the Industrial Revolution, the look of England was in the hands of the speculative builders and the architects. The new rich who were building new houses were only too happy to have their aesthetic decisions made for them by the 'professionals'.

Man's basic need has not changed over the five centuries that this book covers. Apart from the obvious business of living, a house is, as Reginald Turnor describes in *The Smaller English House*, 'a place in which a man can think his thoughts and please his vision'. Every man I have written about in this book, when he had made or married his fortune, built a new house or radically re-modelled an old one in the fashion of the moment. These men were pioneers of new architecture. Since the Second World War, however, nearly every rich man, on making his fortune, has bought an old house and refurbished it in its period style. Why?

TUDOR TO
EARLY RENAISSANCE

Some houses of this time still have a fortified and military feeling, but most are Gothic in spirit. They were built from the materials closest to hand and so have an utterly distinct regional character. These materials, like wood or stone or brick, also determined the architectural style. During Elizabeth I's prosperous reign, houses and brick kilns doubled in number, fashions travelled and, despite the anti-papist atmosphere, classical decoration from Italy and elsewhere began to creep into the English house, first on porches, then over windows, until by the end of the Jacobean era, the slow transition of the English house from Gothic to classical had begun.

HARESTON FARM
Brixton
DEVONSHIRE

THE MOST forgotten manor farm in England, untouched for three or four hundred years, sits safely impossible to find down miles of private sunken lanes which in the spring brim with campion, bluebells, early purple orchids, primroses, violets, speedwell and stichwort. Wooded hills rise behind this, the quintessence of an ancient English manor house. It has rubble-stone walls and its steeply pitched roofs make the granite-capped chimneys seem all the higher. The projecting porch with its embattled parapet is rendered with local marl and is a late sixteenth-century addition. The house has evolved in a haphazard manner around a simple 'hall' type dwelling of the early Tudor period. Outbuildings, including a fourteenth-century chapel, now a garden shed, appear to huddle round the medieval manor as though for warmth, giving the whole an informal and completely unselfconscious appearance.

The name 'Hareston' may derive from the great granite boulder, now hidden by brambles in a field near the house. These stones were called 'hoar' stones and were frequently used to mark parish boundaries. Hareston is still on the extreme edge of the parish of Brixton. It is recorded in the Domesday Book as a manor, and belonged to one Fratmund until 1064. It then passed to Robert of Mortain, followed by Reginald de Valletort and Edric. In the thirteenth century Walter de Colaford, alias Hugh de Hareston, owned it in conjunction with Ralph de Lyneham. Peter Silverlock, whose father had been a Member of Parliament, acquired it in 1367. (One member of the Silverlock family married Matilda de Langford, whose first husband had been William de Mohun – see page 28.) Hareston then passed through the female line for three generations to Alice de Hareston, who married John Wood. The Wood family lived here for three hundred years until the death of the last male heir in 1743. Soon afterwards there was a disastrous fire during the harvest season, and much of the south wing was destroyed and never rebuilt. Hitherto the house had enclosed a three-sided courtyard.

The Hareston estate was still retained by a Miss Audrian Wood who married a Mr Winter. They called themselves the Wood-Winters. Then, three generations later, the Winter-Woods. In 1824 they removed to a more commodious place at Lower Hareston and let Hareston Manor to a succession of tenant farmers. It was in 1863, when a Mr and Mrs Parsons lived here with their nine children, ranging in age from one to nineteen years, that a terrible thing happened. Within a period of six weeks all nine children died from either cholera or diptheria contracted from contaminated water from the well in the house. Neither Mr nor Mrs Parsons was affected. Prompted by a local superstition that sheep's breath would discourage further contamination, Mr Parsons drove a flock of sheep into the house, where the animals were allowed to roam the ground floor rooms for several days.

PATTENDEN MANOR
Goudhurst
KENT

PATTENDEN MANOR, which stands beside a tributary of the River Teise, was built by the rich yeoman farming family of Pattyndenne and later reputedly became the trysting place for Catherine Howard (Henry VIII's fifth wife) and her cousin and lover Thomas Culpepper. The Culpeppers owned the vast and neighbouring estate of Bedgebury and are likely to have bought Pattenden to extend their property. During Catherine's brief marriage to Henry, Culpepper and another former lover, Richard Dereham, were arrested and tortured into admitting having lain with Catherine before she wed the King. Dereham had in fact considered that he and Catherine were engaged to be married, and this, if revealed at the time, would have invalidated the royal marriage. It was concealed, with disastrous results, for Culpepper and Dereham were executed on 1 December 1540.

The house is built on the site of a Saxon prison, which was still used in the twelfth century to incarcerate cattle rustlers. The Pattyndennes were of the newly emerging class of yeomanry, who with the gradual acquisition of land in the fertile valleys of the Weald were one step ahead of the rest of agricultural England during the mid-fifteenth century. The 'Wonderful Weald' of Kent and Sussex is a bed of clay, which determines the character of what lies on top. Oak trees thrive in this soil, and Pattenden Manor, the archetypal Wealden house of south-east England, was the architectural result. It displays a method of building which was so logical and so satisfactory that it was used from the end of the fourteenth century until well into the eighteenth. The basic Wealden house structure is rectangular and joins together the central hall, which is open through its two storeys, and the cross wings, whose upper floors are 'jettied' (meaning that they oversail the floor below). Pattenden is an especially fine example of this Kentish style because its upper floors are jettied at the back as well, a rare refinement. There was usually a passage which went from one wing to the other and crossed the open hall at first floor level. In many cases the roofs were thatched, but are now mostly tiled. The whole effect is distinctive and familiar. There are thousands of Wealden houses which survive, though few as early as Pattenden. They tend to be out on their own, away from towns or villages, for they were built to stand in the midst of their acres.

THE MANOR HOUSE
——— Sandford Orcas ———
DORSET

IT FEELS almost like Somerset here, where the fields and hills are small, and this intimate and beautiful valley enfolds one of the best manors in the West Country. The village, where three streams rise, is of honey-coloured hamstone and thatch, and the church of St Nicholas with its fifteenth-century tower nestles beside the manor gatehouse, to form a perfect grouping. This is England at its most picturesque, at its most idyllically pastoral.

One of the chief glories of this house is that it has been little altered since it was built around the middle of the sixteenth century. A feeling of peace and calm pervades the place, and the silence in and around the house somehow seems more complete than if one was standing, say, in the middle of an open field. Although the building is of more or less one period, it is still nonetheless a higgledy-piggledy place to find one's way about in, as though the builders had not planned it as a whole but acted on whims and perhaps the need to accommodate an expanding family. There is a narrow entrance passage leading into a hall, which has a carved wooden screen and chimney-piece and is lit by mullioned bay windows facing east and south, with heraldic designs on painted glass in the upper lights. A newel staircase leads up from either end. The south stair winds past the old buttery to the first floor, where levels change in and out of the bedrooms and chambers. A step up here, a step down there until perhaps you reach the door of the room from which, although it is locked and empty, you can hear shuffling footsteps.

Edward Knoyle inherited the manor in 1533, and probably set about building this mullioned and gabled beauty about ten years later around a humble medieval hall. (Nobody knows the exact date, which is probably just as well: to categorize a house like this can take away some of its romance.) There are stone monkeys on the gable tops of the east façade which faces gentle lawns, clipped yews and sloping pasture. At the left end is the two-storeyed, canted bay of the hall.

The Knoyle family were Roman Catholic, and strong supporters of first the Cavalier and then the Jacobite causes. Over the two hundred years that they owned the house their fortunes dwindled until the house was sold to the Hutchings family in 1736. They let it to tenant farmers until the 1870s, when the Hubert Hutchings returned. The consequence of the Knoyles' poverty and the Hutchings' absenteeism over the previous two centuries was that the Manor House had a miraculous escape from Georgian owners wanting to keep up with the times. It remains in the Medlycott family, relations of the Hutchings.

BECKLEY PARK

—— Beckley ——

OXFORDSHIRE

ONE SUMMER in 1920, while staying with the Morells at Garsington, the late Percy Feilding went for a drive around Oxfordshire, and miles up a cart track, purely by chance, he found Beckley. Once you have seen Beckley you are captivated. It is a magic place and always has been. Percy Feilding fell for it hook, line and sinker and ended by buying this, the most perfect small Tudor house in Oxfordshire.

Beckley stands like a beautiful beached ship on the ancient fen of Otmoor. It was built by Lord Williams of Thame in 1540 as a hunting lodge beside the once busy Roman road from Dorchester to Bicester. In the ninth century King Alfred had built a castle here surrounded by three rectangular moats, from which to guard the road. After the Norman Conquest Beckley was acquired by a big Oxfordshire land-owner called Robert d'Oilly, and then, in 1227, Richard, Earl of Cornwall built a hunting lodge within the outer moat, which lies unexcavated in the garden.

Thus the place was already steeped in history when Lord Williams decided to build his modest but very modern hunting lodge, between the inner and middle moat. It was built in the beautiful plum-coloured brick he had used at his main residence of Rycote. Owing to the narrow slope of the site, the house is only one room thick, as compact as can be. Lord Williams was up to the minute in his domestic arrangements. The main rooms are unusually high and light and the sanitary arrangements are most elaborate, with three lavatory flues. Under the three perfect gables are three towers, one containing the stairs which Amanda Feilding, who grew up here, describes as 'pivoting around a central column, all of oak. Though it is the only staircase in the house, so hard is the wood that 450 years of treading have worn no hollows in the steps . . . I remember the fear of going up the spiral stairs to bed, the tapestry billowing along the passage with some hidden killer, creaking of wood. As a teenager I moved out of the nursery into the attic. A long dark room, it has a turret growing out of it with a view of untold magic, looking over the yew garden and the rose garden, on to Otmoor.'

Within the moats Amanda Feilding's grandfather, Percy, grew, and her father, Basil Feilding, shaped, one of the best topiary gardens in England, which somehow completes Beckley as a perfect work of art. 'I had always thought that its grip on me was purely personal,' wrote Amanda, ' – I loved it simply because it was my home – but then I found that it caught other people in its web too.'

TRERICE

—— Newquay ——

CORNWALL

THE ARUNDELLS of Cornwall must have been a very sophisticated family, for it is peculiar to find such a fancy façade of this date in such a distant corner of the land. Sir John Arundell, who built it, inherited a fortune from his father, also Sir John, who had lived during five reigns and served under four monarchs. He was a favourite with Henry VIII and his Esquire of the Body. By Edward VI he was made 'Vice Admiral of the King's ships in the West Seas', and his remains lie in the nearby church of Stratton, where a brass plate depicts the knight, his wife and their twelve children.

His son, Sir John the builder, married his neighbour the heiress Katherine Coswarth, whose land marched with that of Trerice. He had four daughters with her, one of whom, Juliana, married Richard Carew of Antony, author of the *Survey of Cornwall* (1602). He painted this picture of his father-in-law: 'Over his kindred he held a wary and chary care, which bountifully was expressed when occasion so required, reputing himself not only principal of the family but a general father to them all . . . as for frank, well ordered and continual hospitality he outwent all show of competence; spare but discreet of speech: better conceiving than delivering; equally stout and kind, not upon lightness of humour, but upon soundness of judgement: inclined to commiseration, ready to relieve.'

His house faces east, crowned by extravagantly scrolly gables with carved mask corbels at their bases. It is built of Pentewan stone, a type of Cornish Elvan, the name given to the local quartz-porphyry. Pentewan was quarried on the cliff top near Mevagissey and is harder to cut than granite, it does not have that same sparkly effect caused by the mica flakes. The bay to the left of the projecting porch contains the full length mullioned and transomed hall window, which is thirty-six feet high and twenty-four feet wide, with twenty-four lights. There are 576 panes of glass in this one window, much of it original! Inside, the room is richly decorated with a fine scrolled plaster overmantel, dated 1572, and a little musicians' gallery which looks down into the hall through a row of arches set high up in the cornice.

Like most true Cornishmen, the Arundells were staunchly Royalist during the troubles, and the sixth Sir John was killed at Plymouth while charging at the head of his troop in 1643. (Everyone in Cornwall who supported King Charles planted a Scots pine outside his house as a sign of welcoming like-minded passers-by who might be in need of protection. Many are still growing today.)

In the eighteenth century the Wentworths of Hembury in Dorset inherited Trerice, and it was let to tenants. It subsequently passed, in 1802, through fairly obscure cousinly connections to Sir Thomas Dyke-Acland, a phenomenally rich gentleman who owned tracts of Devon and Somerset and built the model village of Selworthy. In 1943 Sir Richard Acland gave Trerice, and his two other estates of Holnicote and Killerton, to the National Trust.

WOOD DALLING HALL

Saxthorpe

NORFOLK

AT THE first bend in the narrow lane from Guestwick to Corpusty there are the vestiges of an old carriageway turning off into a field in a south-westerly direction. Twenty years ago I walked along it, half hoping to find a lost domain, and when I had crossed the small brick bridge over a stream I suddenly saw Wood Dalling Hall sailing like some proud ship above hawthorn hedges and ancient meadows, as beautiful and as Norfolk as could be. When I got closer I found it to be empty and forgotten; cattle grazed up to its outer walls, its projecting porch was thick with ivy, its gardens with nettles.

Wood Dalling Hall epitomises the perfect Elizabethan manor house. It is built in a style which England had made her own. Although those terrifying Latin countries were building in a classical style by then, England preferred her own flights of fancy. The Hall is of rose-red brick built in English bond, it boasts a host of gables on every façade, some straight, some crow-stepped, and some topped by pinnacles. The mullioned and transomed windows are large and light, but its fine, tall, clustered chimneys are its crowning glory.

This gentle stretch of Norfolk is Bulwer country. The church, a mile to the east of the Hall, contains myriad ancient brasses and memorials to the Bulwer family, from Matilda Bulwer in 1463 to Elizabeth in 1742. It was Richard Bulwer who built the present Wood Dalling Hall in 1582, at about the same time as his neighbour Henry Dynne was building the much larger Heydon Hall. They bear a strong resemblance.

Wood Dalling remained the home of the Bulwer family until 1780, when William Wiggett Bulwer married the rather pasty-faced Mary Earle, heiress to Heydon Hall. They chose to live in the grander of the two houses, and Wood Dalling was demoted to a farmhouse and remained thus until comparatively recently. This is how it has retained its gloriously untouched state both outside and in. 'There are five attic bedrooms,' reads an accounts book of 1890, 'a box room, four principal bedrooms and dressing room. A nursery approached by separate staircase, and a groom's room over the wash house. Downstairs there is a panelled hall and fine oak stair, dining and drawing rooms, study, store room and large kitchen.'

Over the last few years the house has changed hands many times. Someone tried to make a golf course in the water meadows; another tried to run it as a pub, and put close-fitting carpets over the flags. It is sadder now than it ever was, and the magic has gone.

WILDERHOPE MANOR
Rushbury
SHROPSHIRE

THE MANY-GABLED limestone manor stands tucked into an open fold between Wenlock Edge and Aymestry in the remote and unspoiled Shropshire valley of Hope Dale. It was built by Francis Smallman, whose initials and those of his wife Ellen appear all over the plasterwork ceilings. He came from an ancient Corvedale family, branches of which were in the forefront of Shropshire life during the seventeenth century – Francis's nephew was a Member for Wenlock in Charles I's parliament. The Smallmans lived at Wilderhope until 1742.

The house, set on a south-east facing slope, was probably built by the local mason who also built the nearby Shipton Hall, for they have exactly the same broad gables and the same asymmetrical front. Inside there is the most beautiful and elaborate plasterwork ceiling in the parlour, where huge intersecting stars contain smaller designs. It was executed by a travelling craftsman whose stock pattern can be recognized at other local houses. There are shields in several places bearing the motto 'Droi Deu est mal meu', roughly translated from the Old French as 'Lawful right is ill moved'.

This was certainly the case when some of Cromwell's troops, returning from the Battle of Worcester, called in at Wilderhope because they knew that Thomas Smallman, a major in the Royalist army, would still be away. They carried away what they could on their horses in the form of silver and pewter. When the Major returned and discovered what they had done, he galloped off and, knowing the country, was able to overtake the thieves on the road to Ludlow, where he killed most of them and retrieved his property.

Later on during the Civil War the Major was carrying dispatches from Bridgnorth to Shrewsbury when he was captured by Cromwell's troops. They took him back to his own house and shut him upstairs while they sat below and deliberated what to do with him. He managed to escape (probably through the garderobe flue which is accessible on the attic and first floors), and rode off. The soldiers heard the clattering hooves and sped after him. They caught up with him a mile or so away at the Plough Inn. In order to escape, the Major turned off the road and kicked his horse on over Wenlock Edge. A crab-apple tree broke his fall, and he was able to hang on to it, but his horse fell below and was killed. He eventually escaped and delivered the dispatches to Shrewsbury. To this day the spot is known as 'The Major's Leap'.

THE LEY
Weobly
HEREFORDSHIRE

HEREFORDSHIRE IS little spoiled. Its hedged fields are sprinkled with oak trees, and apple orchards and half-timbered houses abound. Weobly, lying among gentle hills, its church spire visible from miles away, boasts more and finer black and white medieval houses than anywhere in the county.

Three-quarters of a mile south of the church, down a bumpy farm track which was once a well used road, is the greatest beauty of all, a silvery oak-timbered house called The Ley. Since 1589, this house has hardly changed at all. It is built on the 'H' plan with the cross wings at the east and west ends of this north-facing front. Its box frame construction is a method still used in house building today. There is a moulded beam between the two main storeys and extremely pretty carved barge boards on all its seven gables. Above the front door there are two carved panels showing the date and impaled shield of The Ley's builder, James Brydges.

The Brydges family had owned the property since 1428, when their ancestor Symon de Brugge bought it from the two daughters and co-heiresses of Richard de Ley. During the sixteenth century the Brydges bought up the neighbouring estate belonging to the Garways (now called Garnstone), and at the height of their affluence James Brydges marrried Jane Blount and built The Ley exactly as you see it today. James and Joan had three sons, one of whom became a major in Charles II's army and drowned in the river at Pershore. Thomas, his elder brother, was fined as a re-cusant in 1646, and little by little the Brydges' fortune dwindled. In 1707 the last heir died. A letter from Charles Carne dated 27 February 1707 to his sister who had married 'William of the Ley' reads, 'My poor sister, the last Brydges of the Ley is ded.'

The Ley eventually reverted to the Garn-stone estate and has long been a farmhouse, which it remains to this day.

RESTROP MANOR
—— Purton ——
WILTSHIRE

IF THE Ley is the quintessence of Hereford-shire Elizabethan, then Restrop is the quintessence of north Wiltshire Elizabethan. It is built of glowing limestone, known as Coral Rag, a stone made of the fossilized remains of coral and other shells. Restrop was built at the very height of the great Elizabethan age, when the craft of building began to turn into an art. It was no longer necessary, when building a moderate sized house, to be completely practical and simply to provide shelter – people had more money and thus concentrated more on pleasing their eye.

Restrop is of as perfect and pure a style as Elizabethan houses of this size ever reached. It is built on the shape of the letter 'E', not necessarily as a compliment to Queen Elizabeth but for the satisfactory symmetry it afforded to the most important east-facing front which the world and his wife could view as they passed by. It was built around 1590 for a younger son of the Earl of Shaftesbury, whose family had owned the manor of Restrop for three hundred years. The coat of arms of the Ashley-Coopers (the Shaftesbury family name) is over the door, and it is very unlikely that such a very fine house, with its particularly beautiful roofs over the projecting bays, would have been built for a tenant farmer.

There is a local story that Queen Elizabeth spent a night here; what is certain is that she passed on this road on her way from Burderop

to Cirencester. No records remain as to who lived here through the seventeenth century, when during the Civil War a bloody battle took place on the Manor's doorstep. Human skeletons and a cannon-ball weighing twelve pounds have been unearthed in the garden, and the names 'Battle Well' and 'Battle Cottages', both found close by, are unlikely to have been called this without good reason. Perhaps Lord Ashley-Cooper was so horrified that he moved to another property, for there is evidence that the Manor reverted to being a tenanted farmhouse and remained thus until it was sold by the Shaftesburys in 1912 to Colonel Canning. The latter set about restoring its decrepit but largely unaltered state, uncovering the great stone fireplace in the hall. He commanded a batallion in Gallipoli during the famous evacuation of the Arabian desert, and was awarded the CMG. Restrop has since changed hands.

The Manor was an important landmark during the annual and ancient custom called the 'perambulation of Purton', during Rogation Tide in May, when a large procession, headed by the clergyman, would beat the bounds over a period of two days. This was a way of defining the parish boundary, and every half mile or so gospels would be read and a cross erected. Trees like Greenhill Oak and Charnham Oak became landmarks, as did the triangle of grass in front of the Manor.

MANOR FARM HAMMOON
——— Sturminster Newton ———
DORSET

Lost among apple orchards and water meadows beside the River Stour not far from Shaftesbury lies the well settled hamlet of Hammoon. As you turn the corner towards the church of St Mary, which was enthusiastically restored in the picturesque style during the nineteenth century, you are bowled over by the beauty of this grandest of farms. Peaceful, mellow and noble, in the shade of a great sycamore, it is the sort of house that feels as though it has been there from time immemorial.

Once, in a former guise, it was the manor of William de Moion, a mighty man of mettle. 'He came to England with the conqueror,' says Hutchins in his *History of Dorset,* 'with a retinue of forty seven knights of note. For this great service he obtained eleven manors in this county; also the castle of Dunster in Somerset, and fifty-five other manors'. Thus the name Hammoon derives from 'ham', or dwelling place, of the Moion family (subsequently Mohun and eventually Moon. There are still Moons in Dorset). Out of his manors, William chose to reside at Hammoon, and his descendants certainly lived here until the seventeenth century. Romance and mystery were added to the place when Meade Falkner wrote *Moonfleet,* the classic children's adventure story which was loosely based on this family and hamlet, though set nearer to the sea.

The house is built on an 'L' shape, and though it evolved gradually over the fifteenth, sixteenth and seventeenth centuries, the whole gives a uniquely harmonious appearance, which must stem from the use all those years ago of essentially local materials which cannot but blend. The bulk of the building is in Marnhull stone, quarried locally and much used in local villages such as Buckthorn Weston, Todber and West Orchard. However, it was obviously not deemed grand enough by the Moon of the manor at the beginning of the seventeenth century who built on the exquisite Renaissance porch in Purbeck limestone. It is rare for a house of this size and date to remain thatched, for so often the roof pitch would be changed to accommodate the more convenient slates or tiles. A house of this size could take two men six months to thatch, and it might need to be re-ridged every five years or so and re-thatched every twenty to thirty years.

WATERSTON MANOR
——— Charminster ———
DORSET

'BY DAYLIGHT, the bower of Oak's new-found mistress Bathsheba Everdene presented itself as a hoary building of the Jacobean stage of Classical Renaissance as regards its architecture, and of a proportion which tells at a glance that, as is frequently the case, it has once been the manorial hall on a small estate ...' So wrote Thomas Hardy about Waterston, the model for Bathsheba's house in his famous novel *Far from the Madding Crowd*. He describes its every blind arched chimney and fluted pilaster.

There is much argument over the exact dates of Waterston. I can't see that it matters, for the fact remains that it exemplifies the very finest and most elegant architecture which displays the first burgeoning of the English Renaissance. This was the time when the old style of gabled manor was feeling the first breath of classical ideas. The mixture of the two styles is magically uncontrived at Waterston, set now in its cosy Edwardian garden laid out with great vision by Morley Horder, the architect who was helping to remodel the interior in 1911.

Waterston's history is perhaps more chequered than that of the average English manor house. It was kicked around like a football from family to family, none of whom seemed to have loved it or to have been able to hold on to it for long. In 1863 it was all but gutted by a disastrous fire, but mercifully the ashlar-faced east façade remained entirely intact with its projected balustraded bay, its shell-headed niches, its eccentric demonstration of Doric, Ionic and Corinthian columns in three tiers – all in Purbeck stone.

In ancient times the manor had belonged to the Martyns before they left for Athelhampton. From 1377, through various marriages and generations, Waterston passed from the Newburghs to the Marneys to Lord Howard of Bindon, who married the East Lulworth heiress. It was the Howards who were responsible for the daring architectural refinements of the late sixteenth and very early seventeenth century. Elizabethan builders were learning new things from the Netherlands, and Thomas Howard was eager to display his knowledge of architectural fashion. In 1605 Waterston passed to Thomas's kinsman the Earl of Suffolk, who never lived there. He sold it to Sir John Strangways, a member of the Illchester family, in 1641; four years later, however, the manor passed on yet again to another Illchester in part payment for fines imposed on poor Strangways for malignancy, a crime for which he was put in the Tower. From then onwards Waterston stayed in Illchester ownership for two and a half centuries but, since they preferred the grandeur of Melbury, it soon degenerated into the farm that it was in Bathsheba Everdene's time. It was Captain Carter who bought the house at the beginning of this century, and lovingly restored what is here today.

ALLERTHORPE HALL

Gatenby

YORKSHIRE

ALLERTHORPE HALL has always stood apart and important on the flat plain beside the Roman road that runs straight as a die from Borough Bridge to Catterick, and on the bendiest of bends in the River Swale. There is no village now, but for a thousand years there has been a manor. Before the Norman conquest Allerthorpe (which once was Erlev-estrop or Herlevestorp, then Arlathorp) was owned by Count Alan, and his tenant was called Ribald. The place then passed to the Middlehams, and in 1270 was left by Ranulf Middleham to his daughter Joan, through whom it came to the Nevills of neighbouring Swainby. During all this time the Lascelles family, beginning with William, were the tenants. They stayed at Allerthorpe for three hundred years, after which, in 1590, Sir Thomas Lascelles conveyed the manor to William Robinson.

It was Robinson, an alderman of the city of York, who built the present Hall, as a home and, more importantly, as a place to entertain his fellow aldermen in style. The Mayors of York would often stay and hunt here, but the glory was short-lived, for William died eight years after he had built the house. Robinson's rusticated gate piers are as grand as anything in York, from where he obviously employed his stonemason. The house is also exceptional. It is built of the typical pale Yorkshire brick with local stone dressings. The two circular towers still have the original casement windows with leaded panes. There is also one of the original mullioned windows in the main block of the house, but the others were converted into sash windows in the eighteenth and nineteenth centuries. Inside, two of the main rooms contain the original panelling, and above one of the fireplaces there is a fine overmantel with Ionic pilasters flanking carved arches and supporting a frieze with anthemion and acanthus patterns. The ten diagonal chimneys rising from the steep pantiled roof are the finishing touch, making Allerthorpe as grand a farmhouse as you could find in all Yorkshire.

HAGGE FARM
——— Nether Handley, Staveley ———
DERBYSHIRE

MORE THAN any other county, Derbyshire seems to have the sharpest contrasts between urban and rural surroundings. Within seconds black streets give way to walled farmland. Heading north from Chesterfield on the road to Dronfield, with urban sprawl spreading its way along the valley of the River Drone, you would hardly guess that high on Barrow Hill a mile away stands Hagge Farm, as lost and as completely rural as anything in the country. It looks down imperiously towards Staveley, where the vast ironworks used to employ upwards of four thousand men.

Hagge Hall, as it was called, was built as a dower house and shooting box for Sir Peter Freschville, whose main residence at Staveley Hall did not afford such huge views. The ladies would stand on the leaded roof of the projecting porch and watch the hunt run fromNether Handley to Apperknowle, or from Butchersick Farm to Moortop Farm.

The house is North Country Jacobean, as solid and safe as could be. The windows of early houses get smaller as you travel north and the weather gets colder. Here they are half-way to becoming like the tiny windows of farms in Cumberland where fierce winds blow. 'The Hagge', as it is referred to locally, is built of Millstone Grit, so called because being hard and tough it was used to crush the corn in Pennine village mills. Its common name is Darley Dale sandstone, of which there were over a dozen local quarries, some of Roman origin. Alec Clifton-Taylor describes this stone as being 'absolutely dependable', which is how I would also describe 'The Hagge'.

Inside, the forty-two solid oak steps which lead to the top of the house are all original, as is much of the panelling. The ghost of Hagge Hall is a typical 'white lady haunting'. Her spectre is reputed to be that of Frances Culpepper, daughter of Lord John Freschville. She has been seen several times over the years. On one occasion an Irish visitor asked a late tenant, Mr Crawshaw, if the lady in white who had passed him on the stairs would be coming down to breakfast soon. Mr Crawshaw replied that there was no lady staying in the house.

The estate was sold a long time ago to the Dukes of Devonshire and was tenanted at one time by the Reverend Thomas Fosbroke, the celebrated antiquary.

PARHAM OLD HALL
Parham
SUFFOLK

'I HAVE received vague but disquieting information about the inaccessibility of the Willoughbys' old home,' wrote William Dutt in 1914, who was keen to see Parham Old Hall (or the Moat Hall as it is sometimes called), before nightfall. 'It has been described to me as an isolated house in the midst of fields, through which are only rough and rutty waggon tracks, and I have been told too, that it is hidden from passers along the road by a dark grove of trees. . . . Crossing a wooden foot bridge to the right of the village street, passing the village church and climbing a rather steep hill, on the crest of which the road curves to the right, I soon see the cart-track which leads to the hall. I have heard that the house is inhabited, and that it is now a farmhouse; but not a human being in sight anywhere near it; the ploughmen have left the fields, the farm buildings are deserted. Although the trees are still leafless, I do not get a glimpse of the hall until it is within a stone's throw, so hidden is it by a dense screen of boughs and underwood; but I know it is near at hand, for an ancient archway spans the path leading to the farmyard, and just beyond the Tudor gateway bearing several clear-cut coats of arms. Through the arch too, I see the dark water of a deep wide moat; so dark, indeed, is the water that it might well have remained unstirred since the days of the "brave Lord Willoughby".'

Little has changed. There is still an air of past glory, of semi-decay. The Tudor chimney-stacks and beautiful brickwork are the vestiges of a much larger house – the ancient seat of the Willoughbys. This remaining wing was built in about 1640, a time when local builders were more than ever turning their craft into a conscious art.

A hundred years before, Katharine, whose father was lord of Parham, married first the Earl of Suffolk, who died, and then Richard Bertie, who was a victim of Queen Mary's persecution of the protestants. They fled to the low countries, fell among thieves, and Katharine was reduced to giving birth to her son on the steps of a church at Wesel, even the sexton refusing to give them shelter. On the accession of Queen Elizabeth they returned to England and lived happily ever after. Their son Peregrine became a popular hero owing to his skill and courage as general of the English forces campaigning in the United Provinces.

The fifteenth day of July
With glistening spear and shield,
A famous fight in Flanders
Was foughten on the field:
The most courageous officers
Were English captains three:
But the bravest man in battle
Was brave Lord Willoughby.

RENAISSANCE TO BAROQUE

Although remote rural areas remained unaffected, by the middle of the seventeenth century the rebirth of classicism had begun to transform the face of England. Inigo Jones had started to build the Queen's house, Greenwich, in 1616, and Sir Christopher Wren was building the Sheldonian, Oxford, in 1664. Court architects set the fashion, and what used to be an essentially English style took on a strong foreign influence. Sir John Summerson, the architectural historian, said that Gothic architects were masons who thought in terms of their materials and construction, whereas Renaissance architects were sketchers who thought in terms of paper and ink. Once the transition had occurred, some builders expanded on the square and rectangular theme and added wild, exuberant and curvaceous forms - this is sometimes called Baroque.

BARNHAM HALL
—— Chichester ——
SUSSEX

ARNHAM HALL was built at one of the most confusing periods of domestic architecture in England. In the first half of the seventeenth century the traditional Elizabethan style carried on, unabashed by fashion; then again there was the purely classical Queen's House at Greenwich, built by Inigo Jones, as radically different to the former as chalk is to cheese. Then, somewhere in between, there was this strange Flemish style, which Kew Palace exemplifies, and to which Barnham Hall must be closely related. Some people call it the 'Artisan Mannerism' style. It was the eastern side of England which was most strongly affected, particularly East Anglia where many manors display crow stepped gables. Barnham was built at the height of the period's fairly short ascendancy, when these swooping gables were laid on top of the English traditional style, bringing a strong flavour of Amsterdam to the village.

The Hall stands serene and proud with its pale red brick beside the bronze-coloured Pulborough stone of the church of St Mary. It is set apart a little from Barnham Junction, where the trains for Bognor Regis leave the main line and around which has grown an early suburbia on the flat lands near the sea.

There was probably a nunnery here originally, and certainly a manor since the 1300s, for there are the remains of a fish-pond in the garden. Over the centuries Barnham has belonged to the families of St John, Poynings, Fitzwilliam, Howard, Morley and Acland. Then the Shelleys of Michelgrove, rich yeoman farmers, arrived and built this stylish house in the early 1640s.

The most amazing thing about it is the brickwork, which after three hundred and fifty years has hardly softened or worn at all despite its exposure to south-westerly winds and salty sea air. It is a very hard brick which is finely worked in various decorative details such as the Doric and Ionic pilasters which frame the windows on both the main floors and the elaborate dentil pediment and rusticated pilasters around the door. The brick is laid in 'English bond', as opposed to that of Kew Palace which is in 'Flemish bond'. The sash windows were put in at a later date but the glazing bars still follow the lines of the mullions and transoms and look particularly well.

LODGE PARK

Sherborne

GLOUCESTERSHIRE

A HUNCHBACK, John Dutton of Sherborne, known as 'crump', built beautiful Lodge Park. The Duttons had come a hundred years before to the long straggling village of Sherborne in the archaically beautiful Borne Valley, where Thomas Dutton had built the original house of Sherborne Park in 1551. (This was added to over the centuries and culminated as a gigantic mansion of the early 1830s).

Up the long slow hill from Sherborne, over the main Oxford to Bath road, there are bleak, windswept wolds, flat as a pancake, crossed at this point by a narrow and perfectly straight road. Here the last thing you expect to see is one of the most exquisite small houses in the land; yet here, glimpsed down a short straight avenue of completely inappropriate young cherry trees, is Lodge Park. For a long time the building was attributed to Inigo Jones, something people much enjoy doing. Recently the experts have deemed this unlikely. Apparently it is too old-fashioned and cluttered for the great master to have had anything to do with it – despite the fact that Lord Burlington, the aristocratic architect, was convinced of his having designed it.

It was not designed as a dwelling place in the first instance. John Dutton, a great friend of Oliver Cromwell, was a 'learned and prudent man', according to his contemporary Anthony á Wood, 'and as one of the richest, so one of the meekest men in England'. From 1624 to 1640 Dutton bought up the land round Sherborne

Park in order to create a deer park, to be enclosed by a high wall. Once done, he set about building this lodge to serve as a grandstand, from whose balcony he could be with family and friends and watch his hounds coursing deer across the bare miles. The thin beech spinney from where the dogs were slipped still stands near the Oxford road. The lodge contained a large hall below and a banqueting room above, connected by a grand wooden stair. In 1898 Emma, Lady Sherborne, converted the Lodge into her dower house, built two little lodges to herald its and her own grandeur and to house her staff, destroyed the staircase and made the two long rooms into four apartments.

'. . . there is another park,' wrote Mr Hutton in *By Thames and Cotswold* at the beginning of this century, ' it is isolated and wild with a Jacobean hunting lodge worth all the great houses near it thrown together.' The sculptor mason now thought to have built it, Valentine Strong, whose building family owned stone quarries at nearby Little Barrington, will long be remembered for his witty epitaph in Fairford churchyard:

Here's one that was an able workman long
Who divers houses built, both fair and Strong;
Though Strong he was, a Stronger came than he
And robb'd him of his life and fame, we see:
Moving an old house a new one for to rear,
Death met him by the way, and laid him here.

KELLAWAYS
Chippenham
WILTSHIRE

KELLAWAYS IS a perfect miniature manor house, set in flat fields beside the wide River Avon, which floods the farmland around with the utmost regularity. It is a typical 'hanger on' to the traditional Elizabethan style. Many builders of smaller houses in the Cotswolds clung on to this much-loved style which they had so perfected. The manor is built of 'Kelloway's Rock', a peculiar oolitic limestone containing masses of fossils, which was quarried nearby.

Beside the gateposts to the manor's short straight drive, is the famous 'Maud Heath's Causeway', the only way to cross the Avon in flood. Maud Heath was a pedlar woman who lived on Wick Hill and walked four and a half miles, past Kellaways, to Chippenham each morning. When she died in 1474, she left enough money to build, and maintain in perpetuity, the pavement and causeway with its sixty-four arches. The charity still maintains it.

The Kellaway family gave their name to this house and the now tiny hamlet, when they were the lords of the manor in the thirteenth and fourteenth centuries. The next owner was Robert Russell, a merchant from Bristol who is buried at Bremhill, beyond Wick Hill, and then came John Bagot. In 1500 Sir Thomas Long bought Kellaways, and it remained in his family until 1844. If families like this one were on the wrong side in the Civil War, their property was sequestered by Parliament, but it appears that John Long petitioned to have it restored as his inheritance in 1650, and it was probably he who built the present house.

Though they remained lords of the manor, the Longs sold off the house and farm of 122 acres, and in 1834 it belonged to William Stancombe, whose tenant was coincidentally also called John Long. In 1878 The Royal Agricultural Society reported in their journal: 'This farm, in fact, has all the requisites of a prize farm, and we had therfore very great pleasure in awarding First Prize (in all England) to Mr Long who will, we feel certain, consider it a recognition of the untiring industry shown by himself and his wife in the management of this pretty little farm . . . the arable land is cultivated like a garden, being wonderfully free from weeds. Two cart horses and one nag are kept on the farm; Mr Long employs three labourers, at wages of 15s a week, and 3 pints of cider per day. The cattle on the farm are 38 dairy cows and 1 bull.'

SOUTH LUFFENHAM HALL
—— Oakham ——
RUTLAND

HERE IS the perfect Carolean house, gleaming in golden limestone and sailing above one of Rutland's fifty villages and some of the best hunting country in England. But for the glass in its windows, which originally would have been in small leaded panes, it remains unaltered on the outside. Sir Christopher Wren had already built the Sheldonian, and being the court architect had enormous stylistic influence. The radical change from the romantic picturesqueness of the Elizabethan manor house to the measured symmetry of South Luffenham Hall must have upset many of the more traditional locals, for this house would have looked daringly modern when it was built.

The fundamental difference between this new style and the old, was that in order to achieve it you needed the assistance of an architect. The builder could no longer rely on eye alone; the Renaissance was a time for an order based on detailed knowledge. Nobody knows exactly who built South Luffenham, but it is almost certain that an architect called John Sturges supplied the drawings. He was involved in the building of nearby Lyndon Hall, which is exactly like South Luffenham in every detail except that the latter has five bays on each side and Lyndon has seven.

Architecture taken out of Palladio had been translated into English and published in England in 1663, as had Gerbier's *Counsel and Advice to Builders*. Cultivated gentlemen could, with the help of a very good builder, sometimes get by with a minimum of help from the architect, for these books provided inspiration, theory and practical guidance. Gerbier, for instance, says on window design that they 'must be as high again as wyde . . .' and that their mouldings needed 'the broad brim of a good hat to a travaileur on a rainy day'. The result of this scholarly study often produced tall houses such as this, with a semi-basement to rise above the damp and a stairway up to the main floor to add importance. Inside, the Hall retains most of its original panelling. (A surviving bill at Lyndon gives the price for 200 yards of wainscot at £28 in 1676.)

'It will be handsome when uniforme,' said Palladio about his houses, 'because a building should be like an entier and perfect body where each member agrees with the other.'

THE MANOR HOUSE
—— Poulton ——
GLOUCESTERSHIRE

LIKE SOUTH Luffenham Hall, Poulton Manor is built of limestone, a belt of which runs up from the Cotswolds to Grantham. It is England's finest stone and retains a clear-cut crispness three centuries later. Still in the Wrenish mood, the roof is slightly more hipped than at South Luffenham, and the swans' necks over the door have become a purely classical pediment. It has a quiet rural grace about it and, particularly in this area where gabled houses went on being built well into the eighteenth century, it displays a certain amount of daring.

This has always been one of my favourite houses. On journeys to the Cotswolds, when I was small, we would often pass through the winding village of Poulton. The Manor was one of the first houses my father ever pointed out to me in an effort to get me to appreciate architecture. 'Look what a beautiful house!' he said. On subsequent journeys I would always try to be the first to see it and shout, 'There it is, I saw it first!' Even today I still look forward to my first glimpse of it, after a huge bend in the road, through the gate in its enclosing wall.

The village of Poulton consisted of only seven cottages at the time of the Domesday survey. There was a Gilbertine priory here (the only purely English monastic order), traces of which survive at the south end of the village. At the Dissolution of the Monasteries, the manor of Poulton was granted to the Pagets. Some people think that a Paget built the manor, but

to judge by the monuments in the church (rebuilt by William Butterfield in 1873) it would seem likely that the builder was a 'Thomas Bedwell, Gent.', who died in 1691.

Inside, the house is virtually untouched since that date. There are two rooms at the front and two at the back on each floor, and although you could not tell from the outside, the first floor rooms are a foot higher than those below. Hence the first floor is a sort of *piano nobile*, a recent and foreign innovation which did not catch on for very long in smaller English country houses. I suppose that, Holland being so flat, all Dutch houses needed a *piano nobile* from which to get a better view, and that the fashion came here with the new King William. The drawing-room is fully panelled, with a pair of Doric pilasters flanking the chimney-breast. There are wide oak or elm floorboards in every room excepting the hall, which is stone flagged and from which rises a thick oak staircase with fat bannisters.

The manor orchard has a reputation in the village for being haunted. When the house was empty at the beginning of the century following the owner's death, some village children crept into the orchard and began to collect apples. They were terrified out of their wits when the supposedly dead owner appeared through the gate in the wall and shouted at them to go away. In fact it was his identical twin, whom nobody knew about, and who had come back to tidy up his brother's affairs.

OSWALDKIRK HALL
—— Ampleforth ——
YORKSHIRE

'OSWALDKIRK HAG', a fine belt of hanging woodland which covers the steep side of this beautiful stretch of the Hambledon Hills, shelters the Hall from cold northerly winds. The house sits snugly, 275 feet above sea level, with a view southwards out over a wide expanse of undulating country to hills beyond.

It is rare to find such a fine and architecturally distinguished house, built in the reign of William and Mary, in a remote corner of the North Riding. The last forty years of the seventeenth century were a boom period for country house building, and although many of them were replaced in the eighteenth and nineteenth centuries, Oswaldkirk is a beautiful reminder of the high quality of those houses. It was built to impress, and this it still does, rising from the village which huddles around it. Fifty years later saw the high fashion of segregating house from village. Lords of the manor would either flatten the encroaching village and build a new one some distance away, or build their new house on a different site in pastoral isolation. This is why many Georgian and Victorian houses are out on their own, whereas William and Mary and Queen Anne houses are often in the middle of villages, where the original manor had always stood.

The history of Oswaldkirk Hall follows the pattern of so many of the smaller manor houses of England. At the time of the Domesday survey, it was held by Count de Mortain, whose tenants were the de Surdevals. In the thirteenth century Emma de Surdeval married William de Barton, and their son then lived here. From him it passed to the Pickerings in 1316. Sir William Pickering was Knight Marshal to Henry VIII, and when he died in 1542 he left Oswaldkirk to his 24-year-old son, an extremely handsome and distinguished courtier and diplomat, brave and wise as well, and considered at one time as a suitor for Queen Elizabeth. He died in 1574, leaving the property to his illegitimate daughter Hester, who married Lord Wooton. Their hot-headed Jacobite descendant, Edward Hales, sold Oswaldkirk to William Moore in 1674.

It was Moore's son, also William, who probably built the present house, to match his desired image of the new country squire that he was. The old Hall at Horningham, across the valley, had recently been demolished and rebuilt in this classical style in the early 1680s, and William Moore most probably employed the same builder. His new house, built of hammer dressed limestone, with Westmorland slates for the roof, abutted on to the remains of the original house which he made into a service wing, and on the south side he made the grand entrance. He used the best available craftsmen to make beautiful rusticated quoin stones, decorated iron rainwater heads, bolection moulded panelling and door surrounds with broken pediments over, a plaster ceiling on the landing with swags and scrolled foliage, and a grand segmental pediment over the front door.

BETTISCOMBE

—— Bridport ——

DORSET

Almost in Devon, Bettiscombe is a hidden house tucked beautifully into a bowl of hills which culminate in Pilsden Pen, the highest in Dorset. At the end of a quarter of a mile of rough track it seems on first sight to be a typically humble and remote farmhouse, with its low and unobtrusive policies almost growing around it. Then you notice that there are cobbles in the yard, there is lichen on the golden hamstone dressings, the iron railings keeping the cows from the garden are refined and elegant, and the carved and hooded doorway does not seem to herald the entrance to an ordinary farmhouse. You look again. It is only the size that is deceptive. This house was indeed built for a gentleman – it just happens to be on an almost miniature scale.

Inside, a more civilized and settled atmosphere would be hard to find. You walk into a flagstone-floored hall with a triple arched screen. The quality of workmanship is unsurpassed and everything, from the sumptuous oak staircase with fluted bannisters and fat, swooping bannister rail to the door handles and keyhole covers, is delicately and perfectly made. There are three ground floor sitting-rooms, panelled and with Purbeck marble or carved fireplaces. Each of the six bedrooms has a small panelled closet. It is rare to see a house so little altered. Perhaps its remoteness has been its saving grace, coupled with the fact that by the nineteenth century the Pinney family who had built it deemed it too small and dim to live in and moved to their other house of

Racedown, a mile up the road. (William and Dorothy Wordsworth rented Racedown in the last years of the eighteenth century.)

The Pinneys had lived at Bettiscombe since the sixteenth century, but the first Pinney of note was John, a puritan divine and lace manufacturer. In 1672 he obtained permission from Charles II to hold Presbyterian meetings in the house. John's youngest son, Azariah, backed Monmouth in the rebellion and was banished to the West Indies, where he became a sugar planter. Meanwhile his older brother, Nathaniel, married Naomi Gay (a cousin or an aunt of the author of *The Beggar's Opera*), and in 1694 they built Bettiscombe in its present form around the vestiges of an earlier house.

Meanwhile, Azariah had made good in the West Indies, and his grandson, John Frederick, returned to England and Bettiscombe towards the middle of the eighteenth century and became MP for Bridport. Despite his wonderfully unattractive and humourless appearance, his exotic origins nonetheless gave rise to an extraordinary rumour. The Bettiscombe skull, preserved in the house at that time, was said to be that of a negro slave, so devoted to John Frederick that it emitted the most ghastly screams if it were ever parted from him. The story then went that if the skull was ever taken from the house, a member of the household died. The skull has recently been identified as the fossilized cranium of a white woman, at least 1,500 years old, which probably came from the burial ground on Pilsden Pen.

WADDON MANOR
Weymouth
DORSET

WADDON MANOR is more perfectly proportioned than almost any house I have ever seen. There is an inexplicable rightness about it which makes me want to look at it for ages. This has little to do with a conditioned eye, influenced by architectural orders, and more to do with a basic and instinctive feeling that lifts the spirit and brings about a sense of harmony between the scale of the house and the human frame.

You approach it along the narrowest road which creeps warily on the side of a steep chalk plateau, one step up from the flat farm land which, after a mile or so, tumbles to West Fleet and over Chesil Beach into the sea. There, as though hanging from the green hillside, is Waddon Manor, with its air of vanished glory and its sad seaward gaze.

This east wing is all that remains of a house that was once in the shape of an 'E' without the middle. It is easy to picture how it looked, for the steps and ball-topped garden gate piers to the left of it would have led up to the front door, and there would have been an exact replica of this wing to the far left. Colonel Bullen Reynes, who fought for the king during the Civil War, built the house in the 1690s. During the Restoration he had regained the lands he had lost when the king was defeated, and ended up as a Vice-Admiral of the Fleet. He decided to live in Dorset and chose this site (where an earlier house had been), because it looked for all the world as though, when the house was built, it could sail straight out to sea.

Reynes was an acquaintance of the diarist Samuel Pepys, who referred to him as 'a willing man, ready to co-operate in plans for the Navy', and 'one who understands and loves a play as well as I, and I love him for it'. Being a cultivated man, he built his house in the style of the day. The end of the seventeenth and the beginning of the eighteenth century was a tip-top time for English domestic architecture on this small scale. There was a perfect grace which architects had been working towards through the seventeenth century and which seemed to peak in its purest form at about this time, not without a little Royal influence from Holland! Before this time, vestiges of England's Tudor past were still evident, and some time afterwards the style grew tired, and the proportions lost their perfection.

Inside, the rooms are light and panelled with elegant pedimented overdoors, and it is sad to think that the full splendour of Bullen Reynes's house was only enjoyed by his son and his family for a few short years; the bulk of it burned down in 1704. No one attempted to rebuild it, and the house soon reverted to being a farmhouse, as which it appeared in the film of Thomas Hardy's *Far from the Madding Crowd*. The fine pair of dogs on top of the gateposts of the present-day front door were taken away after the fire and put on the gateposts of a house near Mere, belonging to Bullen's daughter-in-law's second husband, Mr Chaffin. They were recently bought and reinstated by the present owners of Waddon.

CROAN

—— Wadebridge ——

CORNWALL

EDWARD HOBLYN realized a dream in 1696 by building this beautiful house. He was an attorney at law who, when he first began his practice, bragged, according to Gilbert's *Parochial History of Cornwall*, 'that he would get an estate by the law one way or the other. viz., right or wrong, and common fame saith he was as good as his word, in the worst sense. Whereupon since his death by an unknown but arch hand, was fixed upon his grave in this parish this taunting epithet:

> Here lies Ned
> I'm glad he's dead,
> If 'twere another
> I wish t'were his brother,
> And for good of the nation
> His whole relation.'

It is hardly surprising that no trace of this epitaph remains on a lichen-covered gravestone in the churchyard at Egloshayle.

Croan is lost deep in old woodland which feels strange and haunted and is always dark. Up the winding lane from Wadebridge which was once the main road, a large light clearing reveals the house, down its straight grassy approach, as calm and gentle and Cornish as could be. It is built of freestone rubble which was quarried in the grounds. From this same quarry the longest bridge in Cornwall was built across the Camel at Wadebridge in 1485, and it is still going strong. The greeny brown surface of the stone is dappled with grey and yellow lichens, and wisteria and ceanothus thrive on this south façade.

Edward Hoblyn's son, another Edward, married Barbara Hawkins. They had one daughter called Damaris, who married a Mr Kirkham. Damaris lived to a very great age and outlived not only her husband but all her five children. She left Croan and its estate to her cousin, Henry Hawkins Tremayne, son of her Aunt Grace (née Hawkins). The Tremaynes preferred their original country seat of Heligan, near Mevagissey, and during the nineteenth century they made a lot of money, which they lavished on the latter, leaving Croan untouched by architectural fashions. It was let to a series of tenant farmers for over two centuries, until the Tremaynes returned in 1914.

The only inconvenience of the original interior was that the bedrooms all led into one another (just as they had always done in houses past: passages were only deemed essential when the segregation of servants became the norm in the eighteenth century); but this was overcome by making a gallery and rearranging the staircase.

FORSTON MANOR
—— Charminster ——
DORSET

FORSTON IS a tiny hamlet on the River Cerne, which winds down the valley from Cerne Abbas to join the River Frome at Dorchester. Over in the next valley to the west lies the great park and lost house of Frampton Court, the home of the beneficent Browne family who were responsible for the building of Forston Manor. Robert Browne had architectural aspirations. In 1695 he built the west tower on his local church at Frampton, in a mixture of classical and traditional taste, then he built Forston in 1698, before rebuilding his own house, Frampton Court, in 1704.

Although it was embellished in 1750 by John Browne, Forston Manor was already extremely sophisticated for a house of its size at the time, for it has some details that are 'Baroque', a style that often moved rectangles into curves. The use of the term 'Baroque' for an English house is really quite recent, and it simply means the breaking of rules and the taking of liberties with the pure classical style. In Italy, Austria and south Germany the baroque style went wild, but in England it was short-lived and remained terrifically reserved and in character with the nobility and gentry who were to live with it. The way the parapet wall, which screens the attics, sweeps down in a bold curve is exceptionally pretty, and it really makes you want to stop and stare at the house as you glimpse it through trees and across the river meadow from the Dorchester to Godmanstone road.

Forston stayed in Browne ownership until 1827, when the philanthropic Francis John Browne of Frampton Court, who had no direct heirs, offered the manor to the county authorities, together with seven acres of land, as an 'asylum for the benefit of pauper lunatics'. He also left £4,000 for its endowment. Hitherto there had been no provision for the mentally afflicted poor; only licensed 'mad houses', run on a private basis, which could only be used by those whose relations could afford them. By 1832 an enormous wing was attached to Forston's north side which stretched for five hundred feet and accommodated 65 patients and half as many staff. Forston Asylum was one of the most advanced in the country and set a new example. In 1863 another county asylum was built a mile away at Herrison, and Forston gradually became redundant. It was not until 1960 that the gargantuan task of demolishing the attached asylum was undertaken and Forston Manor returned to its original self as though nothing had happened.

REDDISH HOUSE
—— Broad Chalke ——
WILTSHIRE

'IT IS aesthetically always a matter of satisfaction when a notable house finds an occupant worthy of its quality,' wrote Christopher Hussey of 'this outstanding example of rustic baroque' and its owner, Cecil Beaton.

Visiting Reddish in the late 1950s was like visiting heaven. I had never seen anything like it; it felt slightly illegal. The drawing-room walls were covered in blackberry-coloured velvet secured by gold filigree, the library walls were green and gold, and there was leopard skin covering the chairs in the hall. There was a conservatory designed by Felix Harboard, lined in split bamboo and with a lotus-shaped lily pool in the middle of its black and white paved floor. The rambler roses in the garden beyond grew along chains which dipped up and down and swung in the wind between six foot high posts, and a row of strangely shaped lumps of yew, grown hugely out of proportion, ran from the north corner of the house.

The yew had been grown by John Combes in the early 1700s when this house was built, and there had been an altercation about it; there had also been an altercation about the building.

Reddish stands in Broad Chalke, a large and disparate village which lies along the meadows of the Chalke stream. In the seventeenth century, John Aubrey, Wiltshire's first archaeologist, lived in the manor farm, and his name is inscribed on one of the church bells whose ringing he loved so. 'The river running near the churchyard ameliorates the sound,' he wrote.

Originally called Littlecotes Farm, Reddish House acquired its name when it was bought by a Christopher Reddishe of Maiden Bradley in 1599. He and his family let it until Jeremiah Cray, a clothier of Ibsey in Hampshire, acquired it in 1702. It was his tenant John Combes who revolutionized Reddish, on the assumption that Cray would pay for most of it. Some haggling ensued, but Combes, who was originally from Broad Chalke and had made good in London as a mercer, wanted to show his village just how well he had done. He ended up by paying for most of the house himself and what had once been a modest little farmhouse jumped up several rungs of the architectural and social ladder. John Combes was obviously friends with a fine stonemason who would have done work at Wilton House and perhaps lived in Broad Chalke. The end result was definitely a cut above the average village manor, with its pediment thrusting forward, its roof line to match, and the strong outline of the window casing, all echoing baroque.

Behind the oval window in the pediment there is a cock loft, and originally there were two pairs of square rooms on each floor, some of which have subsequently been knocked into one. The decorations would have been very simple and little of the panelling survives. John Combes and his wife lived out their lives in their dream house, and their children stayed here until the 1760s. In the 1770s a wing was added at the back, and once again the house rose up the social scale.

SWANGROVE, BADMINTON
Chipping Sodbury
GLOUCESTERSHIRE

SWANGROVE IS a star of a house; romantic and apart. No roads lead to it. It lies happily stranded across arable fields, beside deep woods on the edge of Badminton Park. It was built in 1703 as a *maison de plaisance* by the widowed Marchioness of Worcester for her son, the second Duke of Beaufort. He did not in fact inherit the title until 1705, but a love of hunting he certainly did. It was for this reason that Swangrove came about. Here in the great saloon, light and airy with its tall mullioned windows facing north and south, its smart bolection moulding around the panelling and its groaning tables of food, the men would congregate and feast after a long morning's deer hunting in the park. They could wash their hands in one of the most glamorous marble basins in England, set in a marble niche with a scallop-shaped roof and with water gushing from the mouth of a mandarin mask. In the afternoon, women would arrive in carriages from the great house a mile or so distant. The second Duke was handsome, his friends raucous.

The scene, without the players, is the same today as you enter the low walled garden with its four pleasing square summer-houses at the corners and its grand sweeping steps leading up to the front door. What I like most about Swangrove is its exotic and inimitable rendering of the local Cotswold style. Queen Anne's reign was a sophisticated time to be building. Most of the nobility were dreaming of classical temples in their parks, or other architectural fantasies from foreign climes, which through the eighteenth century grew ever more complicated. But Swangrove has retained all the details of a local Cotswold house and then exaggerated them. The gables are more pointed than normal, the mullioned and transomed windows more elongated, while the dripstone, such a familiar Cotswold feature, has been turned into a frill which still directs the rain away from the windows. Mr Thomas Sumison, the master mason from Colerne who almost certainly built it, was a genius, for Swangrove belongs to the place.

When, in 1750, Worcester Lodge was built, in a sumptuous style, by William Kent at the end of an axial avenue, the fashionable set preferred it. They had grown tired of giving parties and picnics in Swangrove. It became an occasional residence. The third duke, whose wife had left him, set up a lady friend here; and what more perfect house could exist for romantic visitations?

THE OLD PARSONAGE
—— Buscot, Faringdon ——
BERKSHIRE

HERE SITS, in the sublimest of settings, one of the most perfect houses. It was built at the time when local builders possessed that magic formula for rightness of scale. Above Lechlade, nearer Inglesham, the River Thames becomes too narrow and shallow for a rowing boat to navigate. Here at Buscot it has widened out again, the fair Isis, and the walled garden of the Old Parsonage stretches down to meet it, full of box hedged paths, damask and china roses, with clematis climbing everywhere and Kiftsgate roses in the apple trees.

Adjacent is the small, thirteenth-century church of St Mary, which has a stained glass window by Sir Edward Burne-Jones. He was part of that great brotherhood of the nineteenth century whose influence around here was considerable, for William Morris lived just downstream on the Oxfordshire banks of the Thames in beautiful seventeenth-century Kelmscott. There was obviously a larger village of Buscot here, around the church and parsonage, for the present village lies some way off across the fields. In the 1850s the four thousand acre estate of Buscot Park, with its classical house and its village and lands, were in a derelict state. The whole was then bought up by a rich Australian gold trader named Campbell, who proceeded to pull things together. He grew sugar beet everywhere and built, on an island in the Thames still known as 'Brandy Island', a large distillery to make spirit with the sugar beet. He also built a narrow gauge railway which ran round the whole estate. After his death the Henderson family bought the estate and built model cottages designed by Ernest George and Peto in the village. The church and parsonage became even more forgotten.

So the Old Parsonage remained until the American Mr Stucley bought it from the church in the 1930s, thereafter leaving it to the National Trust. This was the house which leapt into my mind when *The Perfect English House* was first mooted. It is a lot of people's favourite house and, happily, there is absolutely no defining why. Neither the National Trust, who own it, nor the County Listing Department, nor Nikolaus Pevsner can furnish one with anything more than technical descriptions. John Julius Norwich, in his book, *The Architecture of Southern England*, sums up quite simply: 'The Old Parsonage is a ravishing stone house of about 1700 with two storeys of five bays beneath a hipped roof; unpretentious, but in its way, perfect.'

NETHERHAMPTON HOUSE
Wilton
WILTSHIRE

FROM 1907 to 1934 Sir Henry Newbolt, our great patriotic, nautical and sometimes contemplative poet, lived here in this lovely manor house on the village street of Netherhampton, backed by watermeadows and sheltered by the great chalk downs. 'We went to Netherhampton for a year', he wrote: 'the experiment lasted for seven and here we are still at Netherhampton after a quarter of a century.' To the church, local charities and various far-sighted attempts to preserve the beauty of England's scenery Newbolt gave much of his time. But in the ghosts of the house 'we have little interest . . .', he wrote. 'One has long made a habit of beheading his wife at intervals in what is now my study: the other, a lady named Madam Sharpe, drops rings and other small objects into a china basin in my dressing room. . . . I have never suceeded in catching a glimpse of her.'

For four and a half centuries the village and manor have belonged to the Earls of Pembroke. There was a humble house here in the 1600s, rented by the rising Gauntlett family who made their money in clay pipes when tobacco was all the rage. In 1670 William Gauntlett took out a patent of arms at the Herald's College and in 1687 made the manor a little larger. Not large enough, though, for William's son John, who became the Member of Parliament for Wilton in 1701 and subsequently built on this exquisite face to his childhood home. At this stage the property comprised 'three ground floor rooms, and three upper rooms lofted. A hay house, a barn of three rooms, a cowhouse, a backside, garden and orchard.' From John it passed to a cousin, then to his niece, Susannah Sharpe (the ghost).

Mrs Phillipa Grove took up the lease in 1782 and on her death her daughter, Miss Phillipa Grove renewed the tenancy and payed £44. 10s a year rent to Lord Pembroke. This was put up to £50 in 1813 – peanuts to Miss Grove, a formidable spinster who had inherited £10,000 from her father when she was twelve. The Groves were an old West Country family, among whom Miss Phillipa was referred to as 'Aunt Grove'. Her favourite niece was pale, blue-eyed Harriet, cousin, collaborator and first love of Percy Bysshe Shelley. Harriet often came to stay at Netherhampton to catch up on all the 'gossip of Salisbury' and to take her mind off her romance with Shelley, thwarted at every step by her brother Charles. When Aunt Grove died in 1840, she left money to fund the school for poor children which she had founded in the village.

The Gauntletts left a house, the Groves a school and, attacked by a critic for writing patriotic verse when he was neither a soldier nor sailor himself, Sir Henry Newbolt left these lines:

. . . Perchance some looked beyond him, and
then first
Beheld the glory, and what shrine it filled,
And to what spirit sacred: or perchance
Some heard him chanting, though but to himself,
The old heroic names: and went their way:
And hummed his music on the march to death.

BRIZLINCOTE HALL
Bretby
DERBYSHIRE

THERE IS an avenue of old oak trees marking the drive which two hundred years ago led through twenty feet high brick gate piers to this beautiful Baroque house. Now the gate piers lean at terrifying angles, overgrown with hawthorns, and cattle graze beneath the oaks and right up to the cellar windows of the south side of the house; ivy smothers the old garden walls, and Burton on Trent in the valley below creeps nearer and nearer, an enormous and inevitable incoming tide, towards the steep little hill where Brizlincote Hall still stands high and proud.

All the country round about was owned by the Earls of Chesterfield, who resided at neighbouring Bretby House. The third earl, who built Brizlincote, had the reputation of being something of a rake. He didn't talk to his wife, who died at the age of thirty-three, having borne him nine sons. (His second son, Philip Dormer Stanhope, who became the fourth earl, was the famous politician, wit, gambler and letter writer.)

The third earl designed this house himself with a view to it being lived in by his eldest son and subsequent heirs. There had been a house here before, built by the Pagets on land they had bought from Burton Abbey. In 1706 Lord Chesterfield acquired the property and demolished the original house. What he built instead was extraordinary and unique. Before the surrounding land was built over in the last century and subsequently, you could have seen it from miles away in every direction. It forms a perfect square, with five bays on every side with the huge segmental pediments above. The tall chimneys perfect its proportions. It is built of small wire-cut bricks from the local kiln, and the quoins and dressings are all of stone from Burton.

The Chesterfield heirs never lived here; they spurned Brizlincote, and its radial oak avenues and the formal gardens grew up to see no Stanhope carriages bowling down the drive. In 1793, Lord Chesterfield's chief steward deemed it 'an old whimsical house, but fit for a gentleman's occupation'. William Barnes, a distant Stanhope cousin, lived here for a time, but for most of its life it has been a farmhouse, which it remains.

IFORD MANOR
Bradford on Avon
WILTSHIRE

IT WOULD be hard to find a more idyllic setting than that of Iford Manor in its secret valley beside the River Frome, with one bank in Wiltshire and the other in Somerset. The south-facing classical façade was built on in about 1708, just after the house had been bought by an affluent salter from Bradford on Avon called William Chandler. Desiring to flaunt his new found riches he did not want to be seen owning the house which lies behind – a rambling hotchpotch of roof lines and gables which evolved over centuries. He employed a builder from his home town who was well used to the sophisticated style in which the many rich cloth merchants were building their houses. Bristol and Bath were not far away, and this particular corner of England, which was enormously rich in the eighteenth century, was sometimes ahead of London in its architectural fashions.

The Romans were always good at finding a sheltered and beautiful site and it was they who first settled here. The Hungerfords of Farleigh Hungerford, the all-powerful local family in medieval times, bought Iford, which was then a mill, in 1369 and held on to it for four centuries. They leased the mill and its house to a reputable family of clothiers named Horton. The Hortons added on to the mill house, and during Elizabeth's reign they made extensive gabled additions which can be seen best on the east façade. The house was used for the making of cloth until well into the seventeenth century.

Iford Manor was bought in 1773 by the Gaisford family, who owned it until 1853. Thomas Gaisford, who later became Dean of Christchurch, Oxford, was only four years old in 1770 when the great cedar tree was planted which still stands on the hillside walk behind the house. Later he planted the drifts of snowdrops and martagon lilies in the wild garden and the woods. Men of the cloth are nearly always good gardeners.

In 1899, when the house had become dilapidated, it was bought by Harold A. Peto, the architect who formed the famous partnership with Sir Ernest George. Lutyens joined their practice as a young man and was much influenced by Peto, who was brilliant, eccentric, energetic and funny and during the later part of his life became increasingly keen on garden design. He created several gardens on the Continent, including Villa Maryland and Villa Rosemary in the south of France; but his crowning glory must be at Iford, where he has brought Italy to Wiltshire and set it tumbling down the hanger, in a series of steep paths, steps, and terraces where colonnades, cloisters, fountains and well-heads abound. On the fourteenth-century bridge in front of the house sits a spectacularly placed statue of Britannia. Inside the Manor, Mr Peto displayed his eclectic tastes and imported great oaken figures to support the ceiling in the garden hall, one of whom is the figure of St Barba, the patron saint of soldiers but also, appropriately, of architects.

MOTHECOMBE HOUSE

Holberton

DEVONSHIRE

FROM WHICHEVER direction you approach Mothecombe, whether along the winding wooded valley beside the ever widening River Erme, or down the road from Battisborough Cross and through the clumps of hydrangeas, or by sea around Butcher's Cove to its sandy bay and up the secret combe strewn with blue-bells and daffodils, the first sight of it takes your breath away. The house and village of Mothecombe (more anciently Mouthecombe) are as settled, simple and beautiful as any in the land. A row of thatched cottages is strung along the lane coming up from the sea and opens into a forecourt in the front and at the eastern side of the house. Before it is the white eighteenth-century railing erected to add dig-nity and distance to the smart new house which John Pollexton built in the early 1700s. Now a great sycamore shades his granite portal.

From the early 1200s William de Mouthe-combe was lord of the manor, and his descen-dants continued to live here until the fifteenth century, when Margerie Mouthecombe, the last of the line, married Richard Sacheville, a very nasty man who in 1431 caused his neigh-bours, including Foretescues, Combes, Pri-deaux and Treebys, to attack Mothecombe with 'swerdis and bokelers, bowesy-bente, arrewes and daggers . . .' They kidnapped Richard 'and smytinge the said Margerie so being with childe that she fell downe as a dead woman there they let her lye, the which was the cause of the saide childe's deth.' Nonetheless a William Sacheville, presumably Richard's son,

then lived at Mothecombe and his daughter Elizabeth married Andrew Stretchley. Joan, their great-granddaughter, married John Pol-lexton of Kitley. Three generations later, the third John Pollexton inherited Mothecombe in 1700 and proceeded to build what he referred to in his will as 'the new house by me erected'.

A local builder, probably the same man who had just built the beautiful house of New-ton Ferrers, created this simple masterpiece in the local sea-grey basaltic stone, mixed with silvery granite from the moor up over the hill to the north. If ever there was a perfect Queen Anne house, here it is, and perhaps a reason for its extra glow is its delicate restoration by the Mildmay family who came to live here in the 1870s. The Pollexton dynasty had finished by 1747, and from then on various relations spurned Mothecome until eventually they sold it at the end of the eighteenth century to a Mildmay forbear. In 1872 Mr and Mrs Henry Bingham Mildmay found an old coastguard caretaking the house, and its untouched and forgotten quality appealed to their fashionable sense of the romantic. They moved in, and in-vited William Morris to stay so that he might advise them on decorating and restoring the place. Morris's effect on a whole section of society in encouraging the preservation of old houses was far greater than he is given credit for. The later restoration of Mothecombe was carried out by Sir Edwin Lutyens who made no material alterations to the original house but added a dining room at the back.

CROW WOOD
Stokesley
YORKSHIRE

'THE ENVIRONS of Stokesley are fertile,' wrote John Bigland in *The Beauties of England and Wales* in 1812, 'being chiefly in grass and not affording enough employment for the inhabitants, a general langour, as Mr Graves very justly observes, appears to prevail. Stokesley, indeed, possessing neither trade nor manufacturers, has no appearance of bustle or business, and is a place well adapted to retirement.'

There is still a feeling of langour about Crow Wood, lying in those fertile surroundings where cattle thrived on the rich pastureland. It was built to house the younger son of the Emmersons of Easby Hall and to display the style and flourish of a small gentleman's residence. The palest pink Yorkshire brick was used, with smart keystones over the windows and elegant corner quoin stones. It is now a grand little farmhouse forming part of a courtyard together with its outbuildings and set against the prevailing wind from the northwest. Pantiles are the typical roofing material of this eastern side of England. (There was an Act of Parliament in the reign of George I, just when this house was being built, which decreed that their measurements should not be less than 13½in by 9½in by ½in, and these dimensions are still more or less adhered to today.)

Crow Wood is set below the north-western flanks of the Cleveland Hills, with a clear view to Roseberry Topping, a strangely menacing peak rising straight out of meadows and woodland. By the clouds which hang around it the locals can foretell a storm:

'When Roseberry Topping wears a cap
Let Cleveland then beware of a clap.'

Looking eastward, the tall column to the memory of Captain Cook, a local lad, stands like a lighthouse on the purplish blue heights of Easby Moor.

Crow Wood was empty for most of this century, remote and forgotten between the roads to Easby and Ingleby. Only a rutted bridle track, where orchids still grow, led to it by way of a dilapidated wooden bridge over a stream; the oak avenue which once lined the way gradually fell. The house earned the reputation of being haunted, and was eventually sold when the estate of the Emmersons of Easby Hall was broken up.

COMPTON BEAUCHAMP

—— Shrivenham ——

BERKSHIRE

'COMPTON BEAUCHAMP house is a gem privily set in a bosky lap of the bare chalk downs where they meet the fertile flats of the White Horse Vale. It is a pearl of price combining in high degree amenity of position and charm of layout.' So wrote Mr Avray Tipping in 1918, persuading the traveller to take the winding road from Shrivenham (pronounced 'Shrinam' by the locals) and to glimpse down its fine avenue of limes heralding what for all the world could be the Petit Trianon plucked from Versailles and set down here in Berkshire.

At the beginning of the eighteenth century Edward Richards set about remodelling his modest moated manor in the very latest Palladian style. In 1710, while the building was still going on, Edward married Rachel Warneford, of Sevenhampton, near Swindon, and their initials are intertwined on the wrought-iron entrance gates. The new north front was built rising directly from the moat. Once through its portals you find yourself in a courtyard surrounded on three sides by the relatively undisturbed medieval manor, whose mullioned windows have sometimes been exchanged for sash. Look through the south door to the garden and there, across the moat, the formal garden of yews and *allées* stretches towards the downs just as it did when it was first laid out. Inside, the Richards lined many of the rooms with wainscots and the big bolection moulded panels of the time, mostly in the fashionable white wood, save for an oak room on the first floor.

The Richards had an only daughter, Ann, who inherited the house. She became one of the greatest sportswomen of the century and was stunningly beautiful to boot. Men courted her constantly, taking off their riding wigs just short of the lime avenue and putting on their grand ceremonial perukes which their servants carried in bandboxes on the pommel of their saddles, 'duly prepared for an attack on the heart of the young heiress'. She resisted all advances, for her love of coursing far outweighed her interest in any suitor. Every day of the season she would travel in her carriage and six to Ashdown Park on top of the downs, where she would course for hares with her magnificent greyhounds and walk for twenty-five miles. When interviewing cooks (her table was famous), she would ask them first if they liked dogs. 'Remember,' she would say, 'their place in my house is wherever they think fit to go.' She wrote her own epitaph:

Reader, if sport to thee was dear,
Drop on Ann Richard's tomb a tear;
Who when alive with piercing eye,
Did many a timid hare decry.
At books she laughed, at Pope and Clarke,
And all her joy was Ashdown Park . . .

The Craven family of Ashdown Park eventually bought Compton Beauchamp in the middle of the nineteenth century, but never lived there. The house has changed hands many times over the last fifty years.

BIDDESDEN HOUSE
——— Ludgershall ———
WILTSHIRE

BIDDESDEN HOUSE, the last word in rural baroque, was built in 1710 for John Richmond Webb, one of Marlborough's finest generals and closest friends, perhaps most famous for his victory at Wynedaele in 1708. He was very good-looking and fast became a popular idol – 'As Paris handsome and as Hector brave', according to a contemporary poetaster. During the summer of 1710, while Biddesden was being built, he contemplated standing for parliament against the Whig, General Stanhope. However, he decided instead to take up the post he had been offered of Captain and Governor of the Isle of Wight.

Webb's house was a reflection of his self-esteem. Grand but not too grand, and wearing all its medals and trophies to the fore. It is built in two colours of brick, pinkish red and slate blue, and is richly embellished with urns and quoin stones. The general obviously ordered all the new-fangled things that were on offer: 'Oh yes, I'll have some round windows, and some arched ones, and perhaps some half-arched ones . . .' On the north-east corner he asked for a castellated bell tower in which to house the bell he had brought back from Lille. In the great high hall there is an enormous and glamorous portrait of Webb on a black charger, by Wooton. (When this portrait is removed, apparently, which it was once, early in this century, the ghost of Webb gallops noisily up and down the stairs.)

The whole effect of Biddesden is ravishing, and it matters not that no one knows who the architect was. Nikolaus Pevsner gives it a whole page in his *Buildings of England* series, which is praise indeed. 'It is a very remarkable house,' he says, 'from the point of view of English, not only of Wiltshire architecture. It belongs to the Vanbrugh-Hawksmoor-Archer group and can hold its own.'

Biddesden was bought by the Everetts in 1795, and subsequently by the Grahams. In 1931 Brian Guinness (later Lord Moyne), the author and poet, who had lived in Ireland and had been spoiled with beautiful architecture, bought Biddesden, recognizing it as one of the most exceptional small houses in England. It fast became a glorious gathering place for the artistic intelligentsia of the day, who helped to enhance Biddesden further. The artist Roland Pym painted *trompe-l'oeils* of Regency figures in two of the blank windows, and Dora Carrington painted another.

In his book, *Pot Pourri from the Thirties*, Lord Moyne writes, 'To me a home in the country was a gateway to happiness . . . My roots and my family's have gone deeply into the fields and woods which the General must have owned in the 18th Century.'

GEORGIAN

The symmetrical and classical looking house was now reaching every corner of England and by the end of the eighteenth century our traditional, organic and unselfconscious architecture was fast disappearing. Andrea Palladio (1518-1580) the Italian architect, was revered and studied by English architects, who built adaptations of Italian palaces in England, but by the end of the century it was the Adam brothers who were having the greatest influence. They rebelled against the Palladian sense of order and then led a classical revival which heralded the architecture of the beginning of the next century. On a minor, but parallel line, from the 1740s onwards the aesthetic rich began building rustic, Gothick and Chinese garden houses and this picturesque style slowly crept into small house architecture.

EBBERSTON HALL

Ripon

YORKSHIRE

EBBERSTON HALL is Palladian to the hilt and also much bigger than it looks. There is an entrance hall of perfect proportions, which is twice as long as it is square, and leading off it are three reception rooms of great height and elegance. One of these, the former bedroom, is the most important room, for Ebberston was built as a romantic love-nest for the mistress of William Thompson, the MP for Scarborough and Warden of the Mint. They say she never even visited it, but there is no proof of this. The enamoured Mr Thompson made the most elaborate water gardens to complement the house, with an aqueduct, canals, fountains and cascades.

The architect was Colin Campbell, a Scotsman who, having worked as the agent of William Benson, was then patronized by Lord Burlington, whom he converted to Palladianism. He had just built a house at Beverly for Sir Charles Hotham the year before, and Ebberston was a convenient following job. Campbell was totally influenced by the great Italian architect Palladio and in 1715 published the first volume of *Vitruvius Britannicus*. For Campbell, the designing of Ebberston was really a chance to perfect his Palladian dream in miniature, for it would have fitted into the hall at either of his famous houses, Houghton in Norfolk or Mereworth in Kent.

Mr Thompson was a bachelor, on whose death the Hothams bought Ebberston. In 1807 Yorkshire's famous Squire Osbaldeston moved here. A sportsman legendary both during and after his lifetime he was an unsurpassed master of hounds and once, for a bet, he rode two hundred miles in nine hours, on fifty horses (each going four miles). He killed a hundred pheasants with a hundred shots at his friend Sir Richard Sutton's estate of Lyndford, and in Scotland 97 grouse with 97 shots. With Richard Hill of Thornton he killed 20 brace of partridges with 40 shots. He was, according to a contemporary, 'a compact little figure, often dressed like a jockey, but almost invariably combining the benign aspect of a great sportsman with the countenance and expression of a rural dean'.

'It was a mere chateau in the Italian style of architecture,' wrote Osbaldeston of Ebberston, 'and not large enough for us; but we took it. At a later date I bought the place and built on wings to make the necessary accommodation. I might have saved myself the trouble, as the family remained together for only a short time afterwards; my sisters married, leaving only my mother and myself at home . . .' The Squire had a stud here and built more stables; he fished for trout in the ornamental lakes, grew circular coverts to encourage rabbits, which he loved to shoot, kept harriers and a pack of beagles and of course his favourite hunters 'Assheton', 'Starlight', 'Elmhurst', and 'Shamrock'. He had to sell Ebberston in 1848, thanks to keeping too many racehorses and losing too many bets on them, and he died in London in 1866, cared for in his last years by a kind and well-endowed lady friend called Elizabeth William.

BIDDICK HALL

——— Lambton Park ———

COUNTY DURHAM

SET IN the dipping wooded hills of Lambton Park, through which the wide and tidal Wear cuts a deep valley, this grandest of early Georgian houses looks south down a long wide avenue, smothered solid with daffodils in the spring. Although, in the evening, the orange glow of Newcastle-upon-Tyne hangs in the middle distance and the moan of motorways is blown to the outskirts of its beautiful formal gardens, it remains a peaceful oasis of eighteenth-century civilization, unchanged in its verdant park, beneath which lurk a hundred disused coal pits. Coal had been the making of the Lambton fortunes, and this house, built by a younger son, is part of the lavish evidence.

It has little to do with local regional architecture. Even the bricks are Dutch, having been brought back as ballast from Holland after the Lambton coal had been disgorged from their boats. In the summer of 1721, Freville Lambton spent much time at Seaton Delaval, the grandest house in Britain, which Vanbrugh was building. It is possible that the latter drew some plans for Biddick; if he did not, then he had a powerful influence. Where else, in a house of this small size, would you see such an extravagantly bold style and brave proportions? Inside, the bedrooms are nearly fourteen feet high!

Here stood an ancient pele tower with a half-timbered Tudor house attached, owned from King Stephen's reign onwards by de Biddics, Daldens, Colleys and Bowes. George Bowes sold it in 1610 to Sir William Lambton, who had two wives and twenty-nine children. He fought for King Charles in the Civil War and was killed at Marston Moor in 1644.

By the early 1720s the Lambtons were living in Lambton Castle, a mile westwards, and Freville, a younger son of Sir Thomas Lambton set about building a thoroughly modern house on to the pele tower. (Its walls are so thick that the present Lord and Lady Lambton were able to install two bathrooms in their width.) He brought in Italian plasterers, who were working at Lumley Castle, to decorate his ceilings, and built a wide shallow staircase with elaborate Vanbrughian railings.

After the Battle of Culloden, James Drummond, heir to the Duke of Perth, was believed to have drowned while escaping to France. In fact, they say, he hid in the labyrinth of coal pits beside the river in the park. Incognito, he worked as a ferryman and lived in Biddick boat-house for over twenty years, when a terrible flood robbed him of his possessions and his proof of identification. It was his grandson who, in 1831, enlisted the help of a Lambton, who had just been made Earl of Durham, to prove his claim to the Earldom of Perth. It failed.

Despite the aggrandizements to Biddick, the house was seldom used by subsequent Lambtons, who were forever increasing their fortunes, their titles and their castle. It was only in 1948 that the family returned.

THE OLD RECTORY

—— Holt ——

NORFOLK

THE SMALL market town of Holt near the north Norfolk coast was nearly all burned to the ground in just three hours in a terrible fire during the summer of 1706. Over the next two decades it was rebuilt to include many fine Georgian houses and in 1725 the then humble parsonage was given this handsome new front by an unknown architect. Although Georgian architecture is now so popular and so familiar, its introduction must have shocked some people at the time. 'It represents nothing more nor less than the imposition of the temple architecture of an extinct Mediterranean civilization upon the house design of a northern people', remarks Olive Cook in her *English House Through Seven Centuries*. 'Not only the members of the small governing class but every squire, tradesman and farmer who could afford to modernize or rebuild his house, even the parson, deputy of Christ, lived behind a façade which was conceived in the terms of a Classical Order, entered his home through a doorway deriving from the portico of a pagan shrine and sat at a hearth which resembled a miniature triumphal arch or an altar to the Lares.'

The priest's home was usually near the church, it was not until the eighteenth century when services became more infrequent that it was thought proper for the priest to become established in a big house, perhaps on a distant part of the glebe, and live with much of the dignity of a squire. Certainly this rectory with its five bays, its golden stucco and elegant elliptical pediment and fan light has all the grandeur of a small manor, set as it is a little out of the town under a small hanger of beech trees. It is not typically East Anglian but for its black glazed pantiles on the roof which are peculiar to Norfolk. Ordinary pantiles abounded in eastern England where commerce with Holland was strong and they began to be manufactured in Norfolk around the turn of seventeenth century. Glazed tiles, however, were extremely rare, a fact which the great connoisseur of England's fabric, Alec Clifton-Taylor, deemed 'aesthetically lucky'. Glazing was done, in fact, to prevent cracking by frost and when the sky is blue the black tiles turn a deep aquamarine.

The exceptionally beautiful garden which surrounds the Rectory was laid out by an enlightened early Victorian encumbent who lined the streams with tufa and planted rare snowdrops and ferns along the banks. Perhaps the only unhappy owner of the Rectory was the Reverend Banks who had an extremely unfortunate affliction of the nose which no doctor could alleviate. A quote from a parishioner in the local newspaper of July 1891 reads, 'All the folks was at church of a Sunday morning and Parson he didn't come. Why for? He had drowned himself in the Rectory pond.' The pond is in the foreground.

MANOR FARM

West Challow, Stanford in the Vale

BERKSHIRE

THERE USED to be elms along the lanes around Challow. The old thatched tythe barn which stood end on to Silver Lane just below Manor Farm has now made way for a clutch of modern houses. A second barn, cow-sheds and stable were also thatched, together with thirteen cottages with bulging bread ovens visible from the outside, when the Raines family, who still live here, came to the farm from Somerset in 1930.

This south façade of Manor Farm was built on to an earlier house in 1725. Its segment-headed windows, keystones, parapet and raised centre bay look particularly dramatic beside mud-spattered straggling farm build-ings; a large herd of Friesian cows amble along its eastern wall each day at milking times. The house appears mildly surprised but always dignified.

A fine oak staircase with barley sugar ban-nisters leads out of the stone flagged hall and the south-east facing sitting-room is panelled. Over the fireplace is a piece of older panelling, probably rescued from the earlier frontage. It bears the initials R.P. 1604, which stand for Ralph Piggot, whose family arrived in the par-ish at about this time. Stuart Piggot, the cele-brated archaeologist, was a direct descendant and lived in West Challow.

In the early eighteenth century the Piggot family decided to modernize their humble and rambling seventeenth-century manor and called in the best local builder, perhaps from Stanford in the Vale, a rather grand village

displaying much architectural refinement. Within a radius of ten miles of West Challow there are at least half a dozen houses that look so similar to this that they must surely have been built by the same hand. These include West Hanney Manor, Kingston House at Kingston Bagpuize, Coxe's Hall at Stanford in the Vale and the side elevation of Ardington House. They were all built around the 1720s and all have bold keystones and this dramatic and sometimes swooping raised centre: as though a countrified Vanbrugh or Thomas Archer had been at work.

In 1802 the Reverend John Piggot sold the manor, and it passed through Hattons, Agaces, Ferards and Schoolcroft Burtons; from 1901 until 1920 it was the dower house to the widowed Lady Wantage.

Across the fields towards the downs is the disused Wilts and Berks Canal. In 1947, when the canal froze, you could skate from here to Abingdon – nearly ten miles. At Kingston Lisle to the west of Challow is the famous blowing stone used to call men to battle. The poet Fran-cis Rose wrote in 1855 of how King Alfred

> . . . his blow-stone blew.
> It rent the air, it shook the ground,
> The well known signal flew.
> In village, hamlet, house and farm,
> It summoned every liege to arm,
> Through Kingston, Lambourn, Sparsholt dale,
> And all along the hollow vale,
> It well was heard in Challow.

WIDCOMBE MANOR

—— Bath ——

SOMERSET

WIDCOMBE IS still a village. Though only a mile from the centre of Bath, it has retained a cohesive feeling, clustered deep into the hills between the wooded slopes of Claverton Down and Combe Down. Up a steep and winding lane, on a small brow beside the church, is Widcombe Manor, which must be one of the very finest small houses in the country. It is a mysterious house, even a little foreign-looking, and certainly resembles nothing in all the long streets and crescents of Bath. It makes the work of the Woods, who designed much of that Georgian city, look quite plain. Many people have written about it. Kerry Downes, in his book *English Baroque Architecture*, calls this 'an elevation of great distinction', while Pevsner refers to it as being of 'an elegant design and by an unknown architect'. In fact, this house takes most people's breath away.

A Saxon and a Norman chapel stood on the site of the present church, which was built by Prior Cantlow in the last ten years of the fifteenth century. His monks had a grange at Widcombe, and at the Dissolution of the Monasteries the lands were divided, the Prior's Park being sold separately to Humphrey Colles while the Manor House and its estate went to the rich clothier, Richard Chapman, who was mayor and MP for Bath. In 1702 a Miss Chapman, the last in this Chapman line and heiress to Widcombe, married Philip Bennet, and they lived and died at his family home of Maperton, near Wincanton. Their only son, also Philip, decided to come back to his mother's home to live. The rebuilding of the old manor took place over a period of about five years and was probably finished in about 1727.

Philip brought his young bride Ann Escourt to his 'new mansion', as a neighbour described it, but she died within three years at the age of twenty-four and is buried here in the churchyard. He then married Mary Hallam, the heiress of Tollesbury in Essex. She too died young, but left him a son.

Philip Bennet the second was a great friend of Ralph Allen, who, having made a fortune beyond realms with his stone quarries, began to build the gigantic Palladian palace in the adjoining Prior's Park. Here he entertained the celebrities of the day, Pope, Warburton, Richardson, Quin and Garrick, who would all have spent time with the local squire of Widcombe. Henry Fielding, whose sister lived at a cottage now called Widcombe Lodge, knew the Bennets well. Squire Western is said to be modelled on Philip Bennet, and the heroine of *Tom Jones* on his daughter Ann. Mr Allen was the undoubted original of Mr Allsworthy.

Widcombe Manor, with all its crisp carving on pilasters, columns, quoins, swags and urns, is as fresh today as when it was built – perhaps by the Bath mason Thomas Greenway as it is a fine display of all the decorative details he could do best.

THE OLD RECTORY
Whittington
LANCASHIRE

ABOVE THE front door of the Old Rectory is a plaque carved with a shield of arms inscribed: 'George Hornby Clerk A.M. Rector of Whittington erected this House 1728.' Edmund Hornby of Dalton Hall had bought the living for his second son, and George, being a man of means, decided to upgrade the mean existing rectory to suit his status.

The Reverend Thomas Horton came to the Rectory in 1781, put forward by his friend Mr Charteris of Hornby Castle. Among his young parishioners was Whittington's famous son, William Sturgeon, the physicist who lived in the cottage next to the Rectory and befriended the Horton family. Sturgeon's father John was a ne'er-do-well shoemaker, who spent most of his days poaching fish and rearing gamecocks. He married Betsy Adcock, the daughter of a Whittington shopkeeper, and their young William became an apprentice shoemaker in 1796. By the 1830s he was a revered scientist and had invented an electromagnetic coil machine.

The upper part of the village of Whittington lies on the south-east slope of a steep hillside. Into the slope a valley has been cut by a little brook called the Selletbeck, which runs past the churchyard and on down to the River Lune. The church of St Michael, with its beautiful early sixteenth-century tower, is built within the bailey of a court castle on this strange hillock which rises from the combe.

The Rectory, stands a little below the church on the site of an earlier house, some of which remains under the long lean-to at the back. It has a very local feel with its sandstone dressings, and is rendered in rough cast, a common practice in areas like this where the Silurian stone was weak. The sash windows would have been an extremely new-fangled device in such a remote corner of England. The provinces were reluctant to accept the change from casements, but once they did, the whole look of England's houses changed and the Georgian period of architecture became easily definable. The earliest glazing bars were quite thick, as they were hand cut from solid wood. During the eighteenth century they became thinner and thinner, until in the Regency period they were often only half an inch thick. Measuring its glazing bars is a very good way of dating a house.

SEDGEBROOK MANOR

—— Grantham ——

LINCOLNSHIRE

IN THE Domesday Book Sedgebrook is valued at £8, having with it three mills, sixty acres of meadow, and land for nine plough teams. Its owners were then called Malet, subsequently Lords of Eye in Suffolk. From then until the fifteenth century it belonged to de Burghs, de Clares, the Earls of Lincoln, de Lacys, Lestranges, and by the 1300s, when Sir John Talbot lived there, it was already quite an important property. Sir John's daughter married Simon Leake and one of their four daughters married Sir John Markham, Sedgebrook's famous son.

Sedgebrook is a pleasant village in the flat, once marshy area a few miles west of Grantham, near the confluence of two rivulets. There is a chalybeate spring just outside the village. 'At Sedgebrook,' wrote Willingham Franklin Rawnsley, 'is a farmhouse which was built as a manor house by Sir John Markham when he was Lord Chief Justice of the King's Bench. He it was who received the soubriquet of "The Upright Judge", on the occasion of his being turned out of office by Edward IV, because of his scrupulous fairness at the trial of Sir Thomas Coke, Lord Mayor of London.' He had in fact saved the lands and life of Sir Thomas, who was charged with supplying money to Margaret of Anjou during the Wars of the Roses and had thus infuriated the king. After his unfair sacking he retired here to Sedgebrook and 'lived a quiet and private life'.

This eighteenth-century stone front to the manor tells of another chapter in the house's history. Its formal approach to the north-west of the church, between wide grass borders with their April drifts of daffodils, is the result of the Thorold family's ostentatious display of modern taste. Having properties in Marston and Syston, they bought the manor in 1716, when Sir George Markham decided that he wanted to move and bought an estate in Essex. As soon as John Thorold of Marston had moved into the house he died, leaving no children. A cousin, William Thorold, inherited Sedgebrook, but he died within four years and his son Anthony also died soon afterwards. In 1721 Sir William's half-brother John became baronet, and Sedgebrook's face-lift began.

A master builder from Grantham was called in and created this beautiful and extremely unusual combination of local style and Italian Pallazzo architecture, with its forthright *piano nobile* and its placement of vases and finials. It is more like a palace than a village manor house. The Thorolds, who still live at Marston, kept Sedgebrook until 1928, after which it reverted to its early life as a farmhouse.

ALDERLY GRANGE
Wotton Under Edge
GLOUCESTERSHIRE

HERE IS the perfect mid-Georgian house. A Bristol merchant, of Quaker origin, called William Springett bought Alderly in the early 1740s and determined to turn what was then a small and jumbled Tudor manor into an up-to-date gentleman's seat. Being a rather mean and frugal man, he employed a local stonemason who was well versed in the designs of the great architects of the day such as James Gibbs. This was probably a man called Michael Sidnell, from Bristol, who had carved a memorial tablet in Alderly Church in 1732, and had later gone on to make designs for the court-house at Westbury on Severn.

This west front was thus transformed in the 1740s, with its handsome ashlar face and its dormer windows tucked behind the wide panelled parapet. Inside, a grand and generous staircase rose from a pale stone flagged hall patterned with black stone diamonds. William Springett also built a coach-house for two carriages and loose boxes under a crowning pediment. Whether this was all done in preparation for his wedding is not certain, but in 1744 he married a daughter of Richard Osborne from neighbouring Wortley House. Mr Osborne was the proprietor of the largest of the fifteen woollen mills which wound their wheels in Ozleworth Brook in the valley below.

The front porch was added in 1751 after the Springetts had had enough of the south-westerly winds. From the only letter which survives written by William Springett, one can only conclude that he was a rather unpleasant man. It was addressed to the retired rector of Alderly, admonishing him for past ingratitudes – for not returning a book, for not calling at the Grange when he knew the Springetts to be there. 'So it is,' he ends, 'that when men from low estate are once exalted, they generally are most forgetful of past favours . . . which is now become too fashionable, especially with such who cover their guilt with the mask of religion . . . I have been and still am (tho' I don't want any of your assistance) Your very humble servant.' (The sad thing is that the rector wrote an apologetic reply.) William Springett died soon after he wrote this letter in 1772, leaving an only daughter, Anne.

Alderly has had owners far more distinguished than its Georgian creator. One of Gloucestershire's most famous sons, Sir Mathew Hale, was born in the original house in 1609 – the much esteemed Lord Chief Justice of Charles II. From 1867 to 1894 Brian Houghton Hodgson, the Indian civil servant, botanist and orientalist, owned Alderly. More recently, the great architectural writer James Lees-Milne lived here with his wife, the well-known garden designer, during the 1950s and 60s.

THE OLD RECTORY

—— Farnborough ——

WANTAGE, BERKSHIRE

IN THE early 1920s, one of the daughters of the Reverend Puxley who resided at the rectory at that time, was playing on the lawn, then separated from the road by a thick laurel hedge. She heard the almost imperceptible hum of a Rolls-Royce drawing up, then saw the tip of a huge Havana cigar appearing over the hedge, followed by a red face nestling in an astrakhan collar.

'Tell me, who lives in this house?' asked the gentleman.

'Why, my father,' replied Miss Puxley. 'He is the rector, and this is the rectory.'

'Good God, I must take holy orders immediately.'

Built in 1749 of blue glazed and red bricks in the local 'Wantage' style, it exemplifies the comfortably satisfactory feeling of mid-Georgian domestic architecture. It is also much enhanced by the middle projection of columned porch and bell tower, probably added in about 1840. The chain for ringing the bell runs down the house, through the first floor landing, where it can be pulled if desired, to the hall below. Originally it was used to summon Farnborough children to school, when the latter was housed in the earliest part of the house during the nineteenth century: the low bit on the west side which is now the kitchen. In the 1950s it was rung by my mother to summon my brother and me to meals.

Farnborough is the highest village in Berkshire, 720 feet up in the downs, and straddles the most beautiful road in that county which leads – without a wire or cable to be seen – through open downland to West Ilsley. From my attic bedroom I thought I surveyed the world. The water for washing had to be pumped up from a well in the scullery every morning for half an hour before breakfast and the drinking water fetched daily in a bucket from a communal tap in the tiny village street. There was no electricity at the rectory, and every evening my father performed the only domestic task he ever did in his life – apart from lighting the fires – when he cleaned the wicks and lit the paraffin lamps. 'In the late afternoon,' wrote Evelyn Waugh in his diaries, 'I went to stay with the Betjemans in a lightless, stuffy, cold poky rectory among beechwoods overlooking Wantage.' 'How very Evelyn,' said my father years later, 'to write so readably and inaccurately.'

The present owner of the rectory told me that one thing people notice when they go round the garden is that there are now no garage doors. He removed them when he first came since they would not shut because, as old Mr Abbott the gardener explained, 'not once but twice Mr Betjeman reversed out of the garage without opening the doors, and when charged with stupidity, made the excuse that on both occasions he was wearing a sou'wester.' In the small church across the way there is the most beautiful stained glass window that John Piper ever designed, celebrating his friend the Poet Laureate who worshipped here and lived in this well-loved rectory.

THE LAKE HOUSE
Frampton Court
FRAMPTON ON SEVERN, GLOUCESTERSHIRE

THE APPROACH to Frampton on Severn, near to the estuary of that great river, is one of the loveliest and lordliest in England. You bowl along a wide, long and beautiful village green, with great stretches of park and garden wall, overhanging trees, duckponds and scattered houses on either side. It is called Rosamund's Green. The houses and cottages are of brick or half-timbered, and it has more of a feel of the Midlands than of what we imagine as Gloucestershire. The Lake House is not Gloucestershire either! At the time of its building, no one in the district had seen anything like it before.

There is an entrance to Frampton Court in the long wall along Rosamund's Green (so called after Fair Rosamund Clifford, who was born at the half-timbered farm across the green and whose co-lateral descendants still live at the court). Richard Clutterbuck, who was an official of the Bristol Customs House, built the beautiful Vanbrughian mansion in the early 1730s and soon afterwards set about glamorizing the garden and grounds. Clutterbuck was obviously very cultivated and very ahead of his time, for this was an early move towards romantic landscaping.

The Lake House (sometimes called the Orangery) which stands in the grounds of Frampton Court, was almost certainly designed by William Halfpenny or his son John, who lived near Bristol in the 1740s. Clutterbuck was an architect manqué himself and

would obviously have seen their pattern books, including the one from which this design derives: *Chinese and Gothick Architecture Properly Ornamented*. Their contemporary, Batty Langley, advertised in the *City and County Builder's Treasury* as being able to 'design and build Grottos, Cascades, Caves, Temples, Pavilions, and other Rural Buildings of Pleasure . . . in the Grand Taste', and this is what the Halfpennys did for Clutterbuck. The Lake House is certainly a rural building of pleasure. It is built at the end of a canal and consists of two perfect octagons connected by a passage hall, behind which is a staircase let into another half octagon at the back. Inside there are waving Gothick-y fireplaces, doors and door surrounds. It is built of stone, and there is a little cupola with Gothic trimmings on the top. The 'ogee' line, which captured the romance of that waving 'line of Beauty' defined by Hogarth, is everywhere. The whole effect is original and has more to do with whim and fantasy, rather than the philosophy and scholarship of the later periods of the Gothic Revival.

Mr Clutterbuck died in 1755, leaving no heirs, and the ancient Clifford family have owned the Court and this Orangery ever since. Five unmarried Clifford daughters lingered in this garden under these trees and painted the most exquisite water-colours during the mid-nineteenth century. Their collection of paintings of local flowers was produced as a book called the *Frampton Flora*.

CAME HOUSE

Dorchester

DORSET

CAME'S BEAUTY stems from being built in the palest of pale Portland stone, arguably the finest building stone in Britain, quarried over the down a few miles towards the sea. It is also the obvious masterpiece of its Dorset architect, Francis Cartwright, on whose monument in Blandford St Mary Church are carved a T-square, dividers, a rule and a scroll on which is incised an elevation of Came House.

Just out of sight and sound of Dorchester lies a quiet park on whose rising ground the Palladian house stands, built all of a piece in 1754, though not to the mansion proportions its creator could have well afforded. It is still lived in by the direct descendant of Sir John Damer, who was perhaps so appalled by the building programme of his brother, Viscount Milton, first Earl of Dorchester, at Milton Abbas, that he vowed to buid a small house for himself. (Viscount Milton caused a considerable rumpus when he razed a small market town to the ground and rebuilt the now much admired model village of Milton Abbas.)

Though Came, with its moderate, manor house proportions, may seem on the small side to be set so grandly in a park, Sir John Damer certainly didn't skimp on employing the very best craftsmen in all London. The present drawing-room, which runs the length of the three central ground floor windows and used to be the entrance hall (until the 1840 addition on the west side was made), must have stunned the neighbours with its sumptuousness.

First impressions were all-important to the cultivated Georgian gentleman – the long meandering drive to display the land, the rich pedimented pillars to display the learning and quality of the owner, and then the entrance hall. A fine gold garland of flowers winds wildly in plasterwork around geometric patterns on the ceiling, gold and white Corinthian columns flank the grand double doors, and paintings of Greek friezes by Cipriani surmount the overdoors. This house is aristocratic Georgian to the hilt, and its ostentatious splendour makes the same impact now as then.

The eighteenth century may dominate this grassy rise, but just to the east, under the trees, there is the simple thirteenth-century village church where Came's famous son, the Reverend William Barnes, was rector. He is buried in the churchyard, and Thomas Hardy and Mr Gosse visited the Dorset poet on his deathbed in the rectory in 1886. 'It is curious that he is dying as picturesquely as he lived,' wrote Mr Gosse. 'We found him in bed in his study, his face turned to the window, where the sun came streaming in through flowering plants . . . He had a scarlet bedgown on, a kind of soft biretta of dark red wool on his head, from which his long white hair escaped on to the pillow; his grey beard, grown very long upon his breast . . . ' On walking home it is doubtful that the companions gave a second glance at Came house, described ten years later by Sir Frederick Treves in *Highways and Byways of Dorset* as 'an unattractive mansion in what is called the "classic" taste'.

CHURCH FARM

Stanton Lacy

SHROPSHIRE

WINDING DOWN the road from Culmington to Bromfield, in the valley of the River Corve, you see Church Farm rising above the river in its rich red brick with rooks wheeling above and the steep Stanton Lacy Wood behind. When the river is in flood and the 'Mill Meadow' in front of the house is under water, the only way to reach the village from here is to use the flood path, which crosses right next to the farm on flood boards, spanning the gap between the churchyard and farmyard wall.

Much of the village, the church, farm and the surrounding land of Stanton Lacy has long belonged to the Oakly Park estate, whose mansion lies two miles south on the River Teme. An earlier farm stood here beside the Norman church until the new owner of Oakly built a smart new farm around a small Tudor building. It was Lord Clive of India who bought the estate in 1760 from Lord Herbert (he had already acquired the Walcot estate to add to his patrimony of Styche), and directed his agent to improve the whole property. Church Farm has been tenanted ever since, and from Clives,

through marriages to the Earls of Powis, it came and still belongs to the Earls of Plymouth. The John family were tenants for two generations around the turn of this century and ran a hauliers business from the farm, where they stabled thirty or more shire horses.

There are three staircases in the house, including a great one of oak which leads right up to the second floor, where the rooms are spacious – not designed for servants – and the views stretch to the Long Mynd. The house is tall, like so many Georgian Shropshire houses, and was probably built by a man from Ludlow. Its garden appears to have taken in some of the once circular churchyard, now famous for its snowdrops.

Perhaps the most famous incumbent of Stanton Lacy is poor Robert Foulkes, who was one of the very few clergymen ever to have been executed for murder. After eighteen years of respected service in the parish he caused a scandal by having an affair with a young woman who was placed under his roof. After murdering the resulting child he was hanged in London in January 1679.

DORMINGTON HOUSE
—— Dormington ——
HEREFORDSHIRE

UNTIL 1963, when it was sold by the Church, Dormington House was always the rectory. Its tallness, reminiscent of a town house, tells more of Shropshire and Wales than of Herefordshire. Built of brick in 1764, the rectory was whitewashed at the time, in order to match the small church of St Peter standing beside, also white-washed to enliven its poor-looking rubble walls. The picking out in black paint of the window surrounds and pediment was also instigated by the Georgian rector, and is very much in the Welsh tradition. Nonetheless it fits in beautifully with the black and white timber-framed houses and cottages which are so much part of the county. The sloping wings were originally squared off and must have made the house look even taller.

In 1763 the Reverend Thomas Whickens wrote to Bishop James in Hereford informing him that his rectory at Dormington was in a ruinous condition and asking his permission to build a new one. On 17 April 1764, he finally got the go-ahead, providing of course that the new building was erected as economically as possible. Some of the older building was retained at the back and several of the better quality timbers were re-used in the new house. The Reverend Whickens ended up with a smart little house whose roof was as high as that of St Peter's and which comprised a hall, a small parlour and a large parlour, a study, kitchen, dairy and brewhouse, four bedchambers and two small rooms in the garret.

After the Reverend Whickens came the Reverends Gwillam, Price and Jenning, and in 1840, when the Reverend Lee was in charge, the village is recorded as having 148 inhabitants, and 'The living . . . endowed with the rectorial tithes, with the perpetual curacy of Bartestree united, and valued in the King's books at £4. 6s. 8d.; present net income, £284.' Then came the Reverends Brown and Cope, and it was the latter who in 1877 witnessed the radical and excessive restoration of the ancient whitewashed church to produce what from a distance looks almost totally Victorian with its new little lead-covered spire and shingled bell turret. However, when you get closer, the place feels as ancient as it must be, for the village is of Saxon origin, and has an Iron Age fort.

The church door has a beautiful Norman doorknocker in the form of the head of a feline animal, and there is an interesting American organ, installed in 1924, which can be taken to bits and transported with ease. In the garden of the former rectory are the graves of the Reverend Cope's dogs, with headstones inscribed with the names of 'Black Puffin' and 'Toby.'

MIDFORD CASTLE
—— Bath ——
SOMERSET

MIDFORD CASTLE epitomizes the Romantic Movement in architecture. This was our very own English movement, which many classical purists abhor and consider mere frippery. It did not look abroad for its inspirations. Instead it looked to our medieval buildings, our castles and churches, and to the wilds of Westmorland. There is no referring back to Vitruvius here.

Henry Woolhouse Disney Roebuck was a notorious gambler who lived in Bath. The accounts of his card games are sensational, but the most legendary was when, during a game of *vingt-et-un*, his life depended on the turn of a single card. That card was the ace of clubs and Mr Roebuck won a fortune. Midford Castle is a celebration of that card, for it is built to the same shape, with two rounded leaves of the trefoil facing out across the valley over Cane Brook and Midford Brook, and the third out to the back. The site is suitably romantic, on its precipitous hillside above the small village of Midford, with a bold projecting terrace around it from which the views down the vale to distant hills are still as picturesque as they always were.

Mr Roebuck employed the antiquarian draughtsman and architect John Carter to design the castle, probably after he had seen a design for 'a Gothic Mansion' by the latter, published in the *Builder's Magazine*. Carter had worked under James Wyatt, one of the first professional architects to recognize the Gothic style in the eighteenth century. Whether or not he supervised the building is unknown, but in 1775, when it was begun, the city of Bath must have provided the best builders and craftsmen in the country.

They produced a castellated Gothic castle which is unmatched. There are peep-hole quatrefoils in the parapet, ogee mouldings over the windows, and the most wonderful plasterwork imaginable inside. The main stone stair climbs spirally between two towers, and on each floor there are three half rounded rooms, leaving a squarish hall in the centre with landings above. Thomas Stocking produced the rococo plasterwork in all the main rooms, and in the eastern bedroom on the first floor there are plaster birds flying overhead. The effect inside Midford Castle is light, airy, elegant and essentially Georgian. Tastes change, however, and the Reverend Richard Warner, writing about Midford in his *Excursions from Bath* in 1801, describes it as 'an anomaly in building equally at war with taste and comfort'!

THE CASTLE

Sledmere

YORKSHIRE

SLEDMERE IS the most beautiful and the most important agricultural estate in northeast England. In the 1770s Sir Christopher Sykes literally 'clothed the wolds', a bleak stretch of land 500 feet above sea level, and set an example of how to plant trees and how to create farmland which has never been surpassed. At twenty-one he had married Elizabeth Egerton of Tatton and become the tenant of Sledmere for life. Having planted avenues and pleasure grounds around the house, he then set about the building of farms and the planting of woods. He employed 'the Great Brown [better known as 'Capability', who]... came to Sledmere early in the morning,' as the meticulously efficient Sir Christopher recorded on Thursday 18 September 1777. The two rode about the parish together, and after a second visit Mr Brown produced a planting plan and a bill for £73.10s. In fact Sir Christopher only used the plan for guidance and much of the one thousand acres of trees that he planted was the result of his own great vision.

The new farmsteads were being built at the same time, set snugly into shelter belts of oak, beech and elm, nursed up by Scots pines. Sir Christopher designed most of the buildings himself, but left the design of 'The Castle' to the terrifically fashionable architect John Carr of York, who had been taken up by the Yorkshire gentry after his triumph with the design for the grandstand on the racecourse at Knavesmire. The Castle was built as an 'eye catcher', to be glimpsed from the library window of Sledmere, as though some forgotten castle had been crumbling in its wood for centuries. This was a typically fashionable thing to do at this the height of the 'Picturesque Movement', when romantic thoughts could be conjured in an instant by the sight of a castle, but the reality was of course a different matter. Although castellated and towered at the front, the Castle is in fact a perfectly ordinary farmhouse behind the façade, and its rear elevation is plain and workmanlike.

When Sir Christopher's farms were first built on the high and, in those days, bleak land, with as yet little protection from the wind, the farm buildings were arranged, as here at the Castle, around a courtyard at the back of the house. Another essential element of all the farms was the digging of a dew-pond, for there was no natural source of water. Sir Christopher saw that the 'very important art' of pond-making was well carried out. The castle pond is extremely large, and still never runs dry.

SHOTESHAM

—— Norwich ——

NORFOLK

Shotesham is unaltered; it is as though it were built yesterday. 'The House is fronted with white bricks of the best quality,' wrote Sir John Soane, its architect, in 1788, 'the steps, window dressings, cornices etc are chiefly of Portland Stone, and the capitals to the pilasters are of Coade's manufactury. The principal floor is raised about two and a half feet. By four steps you ascend the vestibule, on the right of which is the eating-room, and on the left the withdrawing-room; a small cabinet communicates with the withdrawing-room to the library; beyond the library is a justice-room; the best stair-case is placed in the centre of the house, and lighted with a large Venetian window; the common staircase adjoins the offices.'

Sir John Soane was miles ahead of his time. While other architects were falling under the Greek or Gothic spell, he steered his clear uncluttered course amid shallow domes and slow arches. Soane was born in Goring on Thames, where his father was a bricklayer and he began his career as an errand-boy. He finished up as one of Britain's greatest and most original architects.

Robert Fellowes commissioned Soane, who was building several houses in East Anglia at that time, to design his family seat in willowy country just south of Norwich near Shotesham All Saints, a village with a winding stream and Dutch gabled cottages. It took three years to build, starting in 1785. The Fellowes family continued to live here until 1979.

Soane's houses were always amazingly practical for their time. His own notes on the plans for Shotesham indicate his great attention to detail: 'Particular care must be taken in finishing the floor of the Nursery etc to prevent any Noise being heard on the Principal Floor.' In his introduction to the published plans of this and some of his other early houses he writes, 'Ornaments are to be cautiously introduced; those ought only to be used that are simple, applicable and characteristic of their situations: they must be designed with regularity and be perfectly distinct in their outlines . . .' At Shotesham there are delicate plaster ceilings and a frieze of wheat-ears and hops in the entrance hall, which told of Robert Fellowes' surrounding acres. Soane concludes, 'I have been more anxious to produce utility in the plans than to display expensive architecture in the elevations; the leading objects were to unite convenience and comfort in the interior distributions, and simplicity and uniformity in the exterior.'

LECK HALL
—— Kirby Lonsdale ——
LANCASHIRE

HERE IN the most eastern tip of Lancash-ire, wedged between Westmorland and Yorkshire, where Leck Fell rises two thousand feet into the Pennine chain and no roads cross, the small village of Leck sits snugly amongst lush trees, as remote and beautiful as anywhere in England. Through the park, landscaped in the eighteenth century, the River Lune winds along its spectacular valley – a valley that played such an important role in the Romantic Movement. In the 1760s the Lake District with its rugged and dramatic scenery began to be all the rage with artists of all sorts, and in their wake, as usual, the dilettanti rich followed limply behind, thinking there must be some-thing in this search for the sublime through un-adulterated nature. Below the Lakes, the Lune valley too afforded all that was truly pictu-resque. Gray and Mason wrote about it, Mrs Radcliffe raved about it, Turner painted it.

Robert Welch, a merchant from Liverpool, decided to buy a bit of it. He had made a for-tune out of the slave trade and wanted to spend it on land. Leck was then an area of bare moor-land with the occasional huddled hill farm, and in the true eighteenth-century manner of fashionable landscapers like Brown, Welch planted trees in clumps and woods to create the most beautiful park. He had no interest in the architecture of what was then merely a rather dull manor house, but kept on improving the estate, which was to give pleasure to the Welch family until the Second World War.

It was Robert Welch's son George who decided to improve the house. In 1801 he wrapped the plain and pleasing ashlar face around what little he decided to retain of the earlier house. He employed the Staffordshire architect John Webb, a landscape gardener at heart, who had done a lot of work locally and came highly recommended. His landscaping at Quernmore Park near Lancaster had been a great success, as was his probable design for Casterton Hall near Kirkby Lonsdale, which looks uncommonly like Leck. Many of the specimen trees which are still in the park were almost certainly planted by Webb at the time, and the elegant arched orangery in the garden must have been built to his designs. Inside Leck Hall, Webb took full advantage of the very high quality mahogany joinery which was available at that time in Lancaster. There are still exquisite doors and bookcases all over the house – probably from the firm of Gillows, who were the leading mahogany importers in the north-west of England.

Leck Hall displays the perfect late Geor-gian style, plain, simple and pleasing. There is nothing bored or heavy about it, unlike many houses of this period. It marks the end of an era, and although neo-classicism was re-inter-preted by the Regency architects, it was never again so unassuming and unselfconscious. In-side, Webb's work was altered a little in the 1830s by George's son, Robert Henry, who chose to replace the staircase.

REGENCY

By the beginning of the nineteenth century houses had reached their greatest simplicity and were often stuccoed and painted. There was a strong and pure Greek revival which happened as a result of contemporary scholars studying Greek antiquities, and which produced severe and masculine architecture. Alongside this there was a great crescendo of the Picturesque Movement with its *cottages ornées* and feminine forays into fancy Gothic and even Oriental forms.

SANDRIDGE
—— Stoke Gabriel ——
DEVONSHIRE

SANDRIDGE PARK commands the most spectacular views imaginable. It sits amid wide lawns and giant cedar trees high above the eastern banks of the wide and winding River Dart. To the south you look down the steeply falling park to where the river slowly bends around Dittisham on the western bank, and to the west a view cut through the trees shows the river almost encircling the Sandridge promontory, its last wide stretch before it narrows upstream to Totnes.

By 1805, when Lord Ashburton's widow commissioned John Nash to design her country retreat, he was a highly fashionable architect. Though his first beginnings in London as a speculative builder had ended in bankruptcy, he removed to Wales and began afresh. It was through his shortlived partner, Humphrey Repton, that Nash made his reputation in society. In the 1790s he was commissioned to build a conservatory for the Prince of Wales, which marked the beginning of a renowned Royal patronage culminating in the building of Regent's Park and the Brighton Pavilion.

Twenty years earlier, the word 'picturesque' had been formally introduced into the vocabulary of society by one of the movement's staunchest supporters, William Gilpin. Gilpin was a schoolmaster and the vicar of Boldre in Hampshire, who spent his holidays sketching romantic countryside all over Britain. 'The rules of picturesque beauty,' he wrote, 'are drawn from nature ... all the formalities of hedge-row trees, and square divisions of property, are disgusting to a high degree.'

He suggested that cattle grazing in the ideal landscape should be any other colour than black and white, 'which make together the most inharmonious of all mixtures'. Gilpin's theories on the return to pastoralism had a profound effect on his contemporaries, and from them, together with much sentimental theory from Sir Uvedale Price and Richard Payne Knight, a distinctly picturesque architecture evolved.

Nash was a forerunner. He was witty and imaginative beyond all other architects of his day. Many tried to imitate him, but none had his quirky genius. His cottages at Blaize Hamlet blazed a trail for a hundred years.

At Sandridge an extensive orangery took up most of the southern façade ingeniously masking the servants' wing. It had fourteen fat Egyptian columns supporting the flat roof, and floor-length windows between. It has now been replaced by a new colonnade.

Inside, the drawing-room and dining-room are of different shapes, with long windows angled deliberately to catch the two main views of the estuary. The main bedroom has balconies over the west-facing stone loggia and the bay window of the drawing-room. The decorative details inside are restrained and classical compared with the jolly and jumbled exterior. The plain staircase is lit by a lantern in the Soane style.

LETHERINGSETT

Holt

NORFOLK

HERE IS an example of the most masculine Regency taste. During the Napoleonic Wars, when people couldn't go abroad, they became more preoccupied with architectural styles. The interest in Greece had started in the 1750s but reached a great climax in 1820. It had to do with romance and adventure, with Lord Byron and Lord Elgin, with archaeology and theory. The Society of Dilettanti, a dining club for Grand Tourists, looked beyond Italy to the fresh challenge of Greece. William Hardy, a Methodist maltster, was swept up on the Greek Revival wave. He bought the eighteenth-century Letheringsett Hall from the Breretons, and in 1808 engulfed it in Greece, adding this south front of giant Doric columns, which were an exact copy of the temple of Delos on Isis. 'Uncle' Hardy had no direct heir, but left Letheringsett to his sister's son, who was called William Hardy Cozens. The latter studied law, became Master of the Rolls and was made Lord Cozens-Hardy,

. . . And even in the summer,
On a bright East Anglia day

When round your doric portico
Your children's children play
There's a something in the stillness
And your waiting eyes are drawn
From the butler and the footman
Bringing tea out on the lawn,
From the little silver spirit lamp
That burns so blue and still,
To the half seen mausoleum
In the oak trees on the hill.

But when, Lord Cozens Hardy,
November stars are bright,
And the Kings Head Inn at Letheringsett
Is shutting for the night,
The villagers have told me
That they do not like to pass
Near your curious mausoleum
Moon-shadowed on the grass
For fear of seeing walking
In the season of All Souls,
That first Lord Cozens Hardy,
The Master of the Rolls.

John Betjeman

FOREST HOUSE
—— Chigwell ——
ESSEX

The Times of 8 June 1838 ran the following advertisement: 'To be let, furnished or unfurnished, Forest House, Chigwell, twelve miles from the City. The house is beautifully situate, in its own grounds, on the verge of the Hainault Forest, commanding unrivalled views over the counties of Essex and Kent and possesses all the requisite accommodation for a family of respectability. Attached are flower, fruit and kitchen gardens, extensive lawn, conservatory etc.: detached double coach house, stabling for eight horses with loose boxes, brew house, entrance lodge, farm buildings and gardener's cottage with about 15 acres of land, and extensive forest rights whereby the tenant is enabled to rear stock free of expense. To a gentleman fond of sporting, or a family desirous of a truly elegant abode within a moderate distance of town an opportunity such as the present rarely occurs . . .'

Forest House is ever 'truly elegant', high on its windy hill. You can see over Epping Forest to High Beach church, over Shooter's Hill to the South Downs, and on a clear day, down the shining ribbon of the Thames you can see St Paul's cathedral. Here in the verdant environs of Forest House is unchanged rural Essex. The elms down Vicarage Lane which once hid the tiny entrance lodge may have long since gone, and the distant kitchen garden contain only Bermudan style bungalows within its walls, but the high Regency atmosphere still remains.

The house was almost certainly designed by the popular Regency architect John Papworth, who did much work in Chigwell, for several different clients. Papworth was both a prolific and multifarious designer. He was a protégé of Sir William Chambers, who saw to it that he worked in every artistic department, including that of interior decoration, before he designed his first house at the age of eighteen. He went on to write many books, such as *Architectural Hints* and *Hints on Ornamental Gardening*, which were invaluable to aspiring 'men of taste', and on being acclaimed as a second Michelangelo by his friends because he drew so well, he made 'Buonarroti' his middle name.

Forest House, with its perfect wrought-iron double-decker verandah, its octagonal dairy and pretty pedimented stables and coach-house close by, was commissioned by an undoubted 'man of Taste', possibly Sir David Wedderburn, who is recorded as building his house at Chigwell between 1807 and 1810.

Benjamin Cotton replied to the *Times* advertisement and undertook to 'preserve the mahogany doors (still in fine fettle), to turn the pantry and store room into a servants' hall, and the brew house and cart stable into loose boxes.' Cotton's nephew William or 'son' as he called him (for he had no children), was a close friend of Doctor Livingstone, who was brought to stay at Forest House in the 1860s. By this time the tiny west wing of the villa had been removed to make way for a gigantic conservatory, which has since disappeared.

POMFRET LODGE

Hulcote

NORTHAMPTONSHIRE

JUST BEYOND the flower and orchard filled walled gardens of Easton Neston (one of England's greatest and most noble houses) stands Pomfret Lodge, which was originally built as a dower house for the widowed Countesses of Pomfret. It looks out across wide lawns to mild uneventful Northamptonshire countryside, and the private road which runs in front of it winds down into Hulcote, a beautiful horseshoe-shaped model village built around a generous green. It is known locally as 'Chapel Village', because the Gothic windows of the cottages have a mildly methodist look.

If Letheringsett is masculine, then Pomfret Lodge epitomizes the feminine branch of the Regency Gothic taste. Very much in the spirit of the age, the hall, dining-room and drawing-room all open into each other with great double doors, so that you could entertain on a grand scale. There is a lightness of touch in the Gothic tracery in the windows (although it is made of cast iron!) and the barge boarding in the central gable is almost like lace compared with the later and heavier Victorian sort.

Henrietta Louisa, Countess of Pomfret, after whom the house is named, was so utterly besotted with the Gothic taste that she even thought of encasing Hawksmoor's classical Easton Neston in the style. Although only the vestiges of her original Pomfret Lodge lie behind this Regency update, it was her obsession with the Gothic that lingered on and produced this pale pink confection. Lady Pomfret had been an excellent wife and mother and an efficient Lady of the Bedchamber, but she exposed herself to constant ridicule in society because she was so desperate to be thought of as a learned woman. Horace Walpole described her as having a 'paltry air of significant learning and absurdity', and added that she was so totally lacking in humour that 'she repined when she should laugh and reasoned when she should be diverted'. This was particularly sad, considering that it must have been Walpole whom she idolized and wanted to imitate, for it was he who built Strawberry Hill.

Later in the nineteenth century the Lodge became the rectory for St Mary's Church of Easton Neston, which it remained until the 1880s. During the last war it was requisitioned by the Navy. Now it has reverted to being the Dower House.

SHERINGHAM HALL

—— Sheringham ——

NORFOLK

SHERINGHAM IS middle-of-the-road Regency. In 1811 Abbot and Charlotte Upcher, while staying at Yarmouth, saw and fell for a farm which was being sold by Cook Flower. The attorney they instructed to draw up a sales contract was William Repton of Aylsham, the third son of Humphry Repton, the famous landscape architect. The obvious introductions were made, and what ensued was to bring more pleasure to Repton than any job he had ever done – 'such a specimen of my art,' he wrote of his work at Sheringham, 'as I never before had the opportunity of displaying'.

Repton was born at Sustead, five miles away, and had long known and loved Mr Flower's beautiful property at Sheringham which so enchanted the Upchers. 'What infinite variety presents itself in this enchanting spot,' wrote Abbot in his diary on first seeing it. 'What walks with my dear wife and little ones! What a spot to educate them and teach them, to the best of my humble and weak abilities, their duty towards God and fellow creatures.' On 10 July 1811, Abbot Upcher signed the contract and handed over £52,000.

In June 1812, Humphry Repton made a five-day visit to Upper Sheringham and discussed plans and ideas with the delightful Upchers 'such a hopeful and enthusiastic young couple, motivated by high ideals and deep religious conviction'. (Charlotte was the daughter of the Reverend Henry Wilson of Kirby Kane.) A month later Repton produced one of his famous Red Books, heavily laced with pastoral philosophy to appeal to the Upchers. Abbot was knocked sideways with delight, and wrote to Repton, 'I am like the possessor of some gem of inestimable value and beauty, concealed in a casket. . . . You have presented me with the key, and I now perceive all of its hitherto latent beauties.'

The site chosen for the house was in a wooded grove, sheltered from northerly gales and half a mile from the sea. They chose bricks of a pale biscuit-coloured variety which were brought by sea from Lincolnshire. The Upchers did not want anything elaborate, and although Repton had been famous for castellated picturesqueness, here was the perfect chance to create simple neo-classicism, which was all he secretly cared for and the conventional essence of those first twenty years of the nineteenth century. He told the Upchers he wanted to 'unite comfort and convenience with elegance but without extravagance'. They had requested of him a single large living room, an ample eating room and 'no useless drawing-room'. The interior is as Repton had promised, simple and elegant with a brilliantly convenient tripartite bedroom for Charlotte, 'the lady's own room or boudoir, connected with the wardrobe . . . and having a *dégagement* or private stairs'. Walls were painted lime green and lilac. Years later Emma Upcher wrote of her parents, 'They found a spot they thought a paradise and there they began to build their "bower".' Sadly, Abbot died of a brain haemorrhage, before the house was completed.

SUTTON ON THE HILL HALL
—— Derby ——

DERBYSHIRE

You can see the ninety feet high Victorian church spire of St Michael (extreme right) a mile away on a small hill, below which lies the unassuming village of Sutton. The hall, settled in the lee of two gentle slopes on a narrow road leading westward out of the main street is not in the least unassuming! Here is an example of the Regency Gothic style taken to the limit. You might expect to find a house like this in some refined seaside resort such as Budleigh Salterton or Sidmouth, where, owing to the wars and consequent lack of foreign travel, the nobility and even a Royal or two were building elaborate holiday houses. The Reverend Richard Rowland Ward, who built the hall in 1821, must have been a desperately romantic character.

There was always a modest manor at Sutton, held at the time of the Domesday survey by Henry de Ferrers, then by the Boschervilles, who gave it to the Priory of Trentham. In 1291 a rectory stood here, valued in that year at £10 13s 4d. After the Dissolution of the Monasteries the estate and rectory came to the Sleigh family in the early seventeenth century, and among other Sleigh family memorials in the chancel of St Michael's is a remarkable Jacobean monument of a black coffin, instead of an effigy, in memory of Judith, first wife of Sir Samuel Sleigh.

Sir Samuel married three times, but sadly all his three sons died within his lifetime. The Sutton estate with its rectory then fell to his two daughters, Margaret by his second wife and Mary by his third (born posthumously to Sir Samuel who was eighty-two years old when he died!). Margaret was married to James Chetham and Mary to Rowland Cotton. The Chethams ran out of heirs and in 1819 so did the Cottons, with the death of William Cotton. So the property passed to his eldest sister's son the Reverend Richard Rowland Ward and it was he and Mrs Ward who lived out their architectural fantasies.

Apart from spending a lot of money on the church, they built this house, where once stood a meagre rectory, and called it 'Sutton on the Hill Hall'. Built of brick and stone, it was once plastered all over, but now only partly so. From the birth of this form of Gothic in the 1740s to its final swan-song in the 1830s, the feeling of romance was ever strong – here castellations, quatrefoil windows, octagonal turrets, even castellated chimneys and, inside, a wonderful vaulted dining-room all added to the charm. What distinguishes Regency houses perhaps most of all is the elaborate use of ironwork, which architects were just beginning to think of using as a matter of course. It had become easier to fashion and cheaper to use.

The Wards' only daughter became heiress of Sutton on the Hill Hall, and married a Reverend German Buxton. (Their descendants, who still live here, changed the spelling to Buckston.) On 19 June 1841 the spire of St Michael's was struck by lightning so severely that it had to be taken down and rebuilt at a cost of £84, paid for by the Buxtons.

SIBTON PARK
—— Yoxford ——
SUFFOLK

THERE IS a haunted road which curls round Sibton Park to Sibton Green. On the bank are the grass graves of two gypsies who are supposed to have fought together till both were killed. This parish has a strange park-like quality, where a ruined abbey, founded in 1150, lies tantalizingly buried in ivy beside the River Minsmere, which further downstream meanders through the gentle wooded park of Sibton. Before the house it widens into a mere where hundreds of Canada geese gather. You dip down the drive from the Yoxford to Peasenhall road across an ornamental bridge and on towards this plain and golden Greek Revival house. The porch is a semicircle of giant Ionic columns running the full height of the house. They are very surprising and daring. Sibton was built in 1827 at the tail end of this pure and severe period of architecture of which William Wilkins, who built Grange Park, and the Northumbrian architect John Dobson were past masters. The style was a perfect foil to the fripperies of the *cottage orné* and displayed the serious character of its commissioner, Robert Sayer, who had just bought this large property and wanted to live in a modern house rather than the older one by the abbey ruins.

By the end of the Regency period, England had produced and patented many different types of external rendering, which today is generally referred to as stucco. Building materials were scarce and expensive in the first decades of the nineteenth century, and stucco could cover a multitude of sins, including poor stone or brickwork. Sibton displays Parker's Roman cement, which was patented in 1796 and which Nash used on most of his buildings. The process involved the burning of nodules of calciferous clay to form a cement which was strong and durable and could withstand damp.

Mr J.W. Brooke bought Sibton in the 1850s. His family woollen business was founded in 1541 and is believed to be the oldest family business of its kind in the world.

BRIDEHEAD

——— Little Bredy ———

D O R S E T

DAVID INSHAW'S painting of 'The Cricket Game' in the lazy valley of the River Bride might make the fat green chalk hills around look too good to be true. His paintbrush does not lie – this countryside is idyllic. Just out of the sound of the sea, it is as verdant and gently rolling as Mr Inshaw's image.

Bridehead lives for cricket. No summer Sunday goes by without a game. Elizabeth Lady Williams, mother of the present baronet, used to field her own XI. In the 1850s a wing was added to the house (which has since been neatly demolished), with twenty-two bedrooms. This was to enable a whole cricket team to stay here with their valets.

The Williams family have been here since 1797, when Robert Williams bought the manor of Littlebredy, which had long since degenerated into a farmhouse. Robert's father came from the Williams family of Herringstone, near Dorchester, and was disinherited for marrying beneath him. Robert was sent as an apprentice to an upholsterer in Covent Garden at the age of fourteen, progressed up the ladder, bought the business, and became a big wheel in the East India Company, a founder of Williams & Glyn Bank and the local MP.

It was Robert's son, also a banker and MP, who in the early 1830s set about dressing up the newly named Bridehead, making a lake beside it and a complete 'model village' at Little Bredy. His widowed mother Jane had a strong hand in all this and, being a pious Christian until the end (she died aged 102 in 1841), was the perfect benevolent matriarch.

Nikolaus Pevsner did not much like Bridehead's rather whacky Tudor style, referring to it in his *Buildings of England* as 'excruciatingly awkward'. It is predominantly the work of P.F. Robinson, a popular architect of the time who specialized in the 'Picturesque' and could translate your dream with ease. After more than a century of classical architecture, the mainstream of which became plainer and duller towards the end of the Georges, it is no wonder that the second Sir Robert wanted to go 'Tudor'. That was what he chose from Robinson's wide repertoire, which included 'Swiss Chalet' style and even 'Norman'.

Robinson still treated Sir Uvedale Price's *Essay on the Picturesque*, written in 1798, as his yardstick of propriety. 'It is written with the truest feeling for the subject upon which he treats, as compared with the sublime and beautiful, and with an earnest recommendation to those who are about to improve real landscapes to study the paintings of old masters,' he wrote. 'The Old English Style' he favoured most was seldom so well displayed as here and in the Bride Valley.

VICTORIAN

By now roads, canals and railways enabled the spread of uniform building materials to all parts of the country. The regional materials of each area, once so varied, began their slow demise as bricks, for instance, became cheaper to import from the Midlands than to bake in the village kiln. A ubiquitous look began, particularly in town and city suburbs. This era was packed with architectural revivals including Italianate and baronial. Most chose the Gothic route, whether it was Ruskin's preferred Italian medieval Gothic or William Morris's and Philip Webb's return to English rural traditionalism. Architects inspired by Augustus Welby Northmore Pugin thought of their architecture in terms of 'morality and truthfulness', which often produced a stalwart solidity in their houses. By the end of the century Richard Norman Shaw had produced a free romantic style.

ST MARIE'S GRANGE

Alderbury

SALISBURY, WILTSHIRE

'THERE ARE only two things worth living for,' said Augustus Welby Northmore Pugin, 'Christian architecture and a boat.' St Marie's Grange provided a little of both. It was a home that the great prophet of Gothic designed for himself and his family, and today it is still as strange and startling as it was when he built it around 1835. Pugin (who designed the Houses of Parliament with Sir Charles Barry), was fifty years ahead of his time. When pale imitations of Greece and left-overs of Strawberry Hill Gothic were the norm, suddenly, on a site just south of Salisbury, with 'a magnificent view of the cathedral and city with the River Avon winding through . . . as advantageous a situation as any in England', there sprang up this towered, monastic, miniature Gothic château.

Pugin was not trying to be different for the sake of it; his medieval revival was born from a genuine moral and religious fervour. He believed that good architecture could only be created by good people and that you could only be good by being an unreformed Christian. Hence everything he built sprang from the fifteenth century and before. Pugin's strict rules and principles were upheld in part to counteract the inordinate sadness he had suffered at the age of twenty-two, when his first wife died giving birth to their only daughter. At twenty-three he married again, became a Roman Catholic and decided to buckle down to work as best he could and prove by his buildings that 'everything grand, edifying and noble in art is the result of feelings produced by the catholic religion on the human mind.' (He found it difficult to come to terms with the fact that the Roman Catholics were responsible for the Italian classical revival in the sixteenth and seventeenth centuries.)

St Marie's is built on a small plateau above the wide Avon, and on alder-strewn, willowy meadow land, but in a somewhat awkward position. For technical reasons the house had to be set back under a steep bank, and so feels slightly cramped. Although the large Gothic window of the chapel was replaced by a smaller one, and bay windows were added a few years later, it is still, in Pugin's own words, 'the only modern building that is complete in every part in the ancient style'.

Within, the atmosphere is heavily ecclesiastical and Pugin's soul still hangs in the air, despite some alterations to the internal layout. A stained glass window lights the stairs, his initials in Gothic lettering appear in much of the decoration, and dark woodwork pervades all. Six months after the house was finished and the specially commissioned green leather furniture from Hull of Wardour Street had been arranged, Mrs Pugin's health proved unsuited to watery Wiltshire.

The house had cost upwards of £2,000 to build, and Pugin had great difficulty in selling it. Nobody wanted such a queer house. He ended up by selling it for £500 to Mr Staples, from whom he originally bought the site for the same sum.

WINSTON GRANGE

Debenham

SUFFOLK

IN 1843 the parishioners of Winston were worried about the dilapidated state of their vicarage, which stood next to the church of St Andrew. The patron of the living asked the architect Samuel Saunders Teulon to make a report on it. He suggested that it had gone too far and should be pulled down. In its stead he built Winston Grange on a piece of glebeland across the fields from the ancient and unassuming little church. It was a bold and expensive move, for the parish of Winston was small and, in consequence, so was the stipend.

The building of Winston Grange, containing the first flush lavatory in Suffolk, proved a triumph, for in 1860 the third incumbent, a Reverend Mundiford Allen, became one of the best and most loved vicars in East Anglia, and although he died and was buried here in 1910, stories of his virtue and kindness are still rife. Mundiford supplemented his stipend by farming the glebeland, and grew two orchards. Among the apple trees, one hot summer in the 1880s, he dug and puddled a large pond with the help of his two sons, which was used as the family swimming pool for years afterwards. On the top floor of the house there were three tiny rooms, one for boxes, one for the Allen boys, and one for the five Allen daughters. When their mother died in 1890, the eldest daughter, who was by then thirty years old, was allowed to move to the first floor bedroom, and from then on she ruled the roost. The maid of all work also died at about this time and was not replaced. When their father died in 1910, the five Allen girls, who never married, moved to Clacton-on-Sea, where they ran a high-class boarding house. Each of the five is buried at Winston.

The Grange has always been a happy house and still has a faint atmosphere of piety, fully intended by Mr Teulon. This was a restrained and early work from an architect renowned for his roguish style, who went on to shock and irritate many of his contemporaries but also to amaze and satisfy his clients. His specialities were country houses, churches and vicarages, and he had a great love for bricks, which he used brilliantly and ingeniously. He did not gain many public commissions, because he did not care for architectural competitions. He looked like the archetypal respectable Victorian, with mutton chop whiskers, a top hat, a good wife, four sons, four daughters, and strong evangelical convictions. It was the latter fact that got him so many commissions from the Church of England, who abhorred the Catholic leanings of Pugin and his stable. The later wildness and eccentricity of his style were completely out of character with his conventional, moral and industrious way of life; his obituary reported that he had died from overwork.

The Reverend Allen's successor dealt in motor bikes to supplement his pay, but by the 1930s the parish had become so small that a vicarage seemed unnecessary, and it was sold.

TOFT MANOR

—— Comberton ——

CAMBRIDGESHIRE

THE ARCHITECTS of Victorian England were now born – Barry, Pugin, Scott, Cockerell, Paxton, Street, Butterfield, Waterhouse and Shaw, and the new age reflected every sort of change from social to technological. The architect who could now travel to sites on a steam train and use technical terms and modern scaffolding had a different relationship with the client, who was more informed about what he wanted in the way of a new house in the country. Whereas architectural changes in the small country house had been slowly transitional in the last four hundred years, so that you hardly noticed the slipping of one style into another over, say, a period of fifty years, now the changes were radical and sometimes startling. If you wanted to rise in your profession as an architect, you would probably choose the Gothic route.

Toft Manor was built as a parsonage for St Andrew's church, which the *Shell Guide to Cambridgeshire* describes as 'gloomy and largely rebuilt, (with) alabaster figures and dreadful Victorian stained glass'. One of the editors of the *Ecclesiologist*, writing in 1845, declared that this house, the former parsonage, 'exhibits a great advance upon the usual style. We think he [the architect] has adopted perhaps too late a period for his model: and there is a little exaggeration in the design which we have no doubt will be amended in the future.' Did the architect get eight out of ten from the powers that be? Samuel Whitfield Daukes was his name, and what a very fine job he made of this rambling Gothic house of flint with its stone dressings, its 'Tudor' windows with their mullions and transomes, and its jolly carved bargeboards. It is typical of a certain sort of domestic architecture which exudes an air of virtue and solidity. Although it may be easier to like the look of a classical house, few imagine how pleasant it might be to live in a Tudor Revival one which combines quaint picturesqueness with modern practicalities.

Daukes was a great admirer of Pugin's architecture, including St Marie's Grange, though not of his high-minded religious ideas; he was very low church himself. He was also a man of means and in 1839, as a young architect, he bought up an estate in Cheltenham known as the Park and set about making fourteen acres of formal gardens and building six of speculative housing. He went on to become famous in the Cheltenham and Gloucester area, where he built many churches and railway stations, as well as Witley Court in Worcestershire, for the Earl of Dudley, and Cirencester Agricultural College.

THE OLD RECTORY
——— St Colomb Major ———
C O R N W A L L

NEAR NINE Maidens, the only ancient stone avenue in Cornwall, the little town of St Colomb Major straggles over a steep hill. It has a fine high street at its summit, 'country grand' Victorian buildings, classical Town Hall, Temperance Hall and non-conformist chapels, and a formidable trio of Bank House, Penmellyn House and Old Rectory, by the curious Victorian architect William White. The Rectory is designed in a simple medieval Gothic Revival style. The random roof lines and the use of local materials enable it to fit into the hillside as organically as White had planned. It is a far cry from the Regency Gothic of twenty years earlier, when parsonages sported wrought-iron verandahs looking on to wide lawns and cedar trees. The new clergy houses were of a quite different, selfless and holy Gothic architecture.

The great nephew of the naturalist Gilbert White of Selborne, William White, was odds on to be a follower of Pugin and one of the 'Ecclesiological set'. He was the son of a clergyman, the brother of the Archdeacon of Grahamstown and the brother-in-law of the Bishop of Madagascar. He carried a prayer-book and hymnal in his 'Patent Alpine Porte-Knapsack' (his own invention, 'said to create no pressure on the back or arm') when mountaineering. He disapproved of shaving, sported a beard to his navel and was a great advocate of Swedish gymnastics. Mark Girouard, in *The Victorian Country House*, describes his appearance in the Alps: 'He wore a flannel suit, brown canvas gaiters and boots with porpoise-hide laces. A puggaree of Indian cotton hung from the back of his hat, to protect his neck from the sun; a brown veil shielded his eyes from the snow; a whistle hung from his button-hole.' He would sometimes sing a song of his own composition called 'Alpine Queen' or 'Mountaineer's Song'.

William White had worked in the office of the architect Sir George Gilbert Scott, during which time he had met the famous church architects G.F. Bodley and G.E. Street. In 1847 he set up his own practice in Truro and designed the Old Rectory when he was only twenty-four years old. Of granite, which he has used in dressings around the doors and windows, he wrote: 'Especial care is required to make the mouldings of a broad, bold and massive, rather than a small or delicately undercut character, and to avoid as far as possible anything like minuteness and pettiness in the finish.' The interior banister at the Old Rectory is of granite and is certainly bold and massive, with ceiling-high columns half enclosing the staircase.

'White spent much of his life balanced on the boundary between crankiness and brilliance,' continues Girouard; 'in the end he fell off on the wrong side, and a large proportion of his last years were wasted in trying to prove that Shakespeare was Bacon. The crankiness should not obscure the brilliance. As an architect he is one of the most interesting and least known of the Victorian Gothic Revivalists.'

HINDERTON HALL

Neston

CHESHIRE

CHRISTOPHER BUSHNELL was a Liverpool wine merchant who decided to move from the city and build an honest, solid house in the beautiful Wirral. The civic grandeur of Liverpool, which in the middle of the nineteenth century was ever expanding on the most monumental scale, must have influenced Mr Bushnell's taste, for he had strong views on what he wanted. He chose Alfred Waterhouse as his architect, perhaps because he was a local boy from Liverpool. He could have had no idea that Mr Waterhouse was to become one of the greatest civic architects of the north, for in 1856, when Hinderton Hall was built, he was still at the brink of his career.

Alfred Waterhouse was born in 1830, the first of eight children. His parents were Quakers, and Alfred's contacts were only among 'friends' until he was eighteen. After a five-year apprenticeship to Richard Lane of Manchester, he travelled abroad for a year and sketched the most extraordinary number of buildings and architectural details. Greek remains in Paestum, mosques in Istanbul, palaces in Rome and churches in Rouen. Two years later he built Hinderton, which faintly resembles a French château mixed very weakly with a Scottish manse. Victorian Gothic it certainly is, and looks wonderfully strong and solid and right for its hard-working and worthy owner, who was not averse to a little picturesque grouping of steep roofs and gables and the addition of a narrow corner tower.

The house is built of rock-faced sandstone which is of the deepest pink, peculiar to this area, and its roofs are of patterned slate. There is a two-storeyed entrance hall, twenty-five feet square, around which are the main reception rooms, grouped informally. The surrounding garden is thick with evergreens. Tall firs form a copse at the back of the house and great clumps of rhododendrons and laurels surround the lawns to the south, conserving the safe, dark Victorian atmosphere of the place. Chestnuts line the edge of the small park and afford the house a dignified protection from the lorries that now hurtle by on the main road.

THE RED HOUSE

—— Bexley Heath ——

KENT

THE RED House is a celebrated Victorian house – built for William Morris, writer, socialist, artist, craftsman and manufacturer, by his friend, the great architect Philip Webb. The young Morris, born in Walthamstow and educated at Marlborough, had wanted something 'very medieval in spirit', and the bit of north Kent which was then deep in the fruit-growing countryside seemed the perfect place to build. In the summer of 1858, Morris, Webb and Charles Faulkner had gone on a rowing trip down the River Seine, to look at medieval cathedrals. It was then the plan to build the Red House was formed.

Early in the April of 1859 the contract on the land was signed, and on the 26th of that month, at the age of twenty-five, William Morris married Jane Burden, an Oxford girl. The newly-weds moved into the Red House in 1860, and began to furnish and decorate it to Morris's own designs. (This was the origin of Morris and Co.) In 1861 Jane Morris was born, and a year later May Morris. Everything was rosy at the Red House, which Dante Gabriel Rossetti, Morris's close friend and mentor described as 'more a poem than a house . . . but an admirable place to live in too'.

It is a house which has given rise to much aesthetic conjecture, and for a long time it was deemed to be the first seed of the modern movement in England, for it did not appear to be built in any revival style, but in a fresh new one. William Morris thought of it as being 'in the style of the thirteenth century', but then it is also in the style of Philip Webb's master, G.E. Street, in whose office he had worked. He had hardly left the office when he built this, his first house as an independent architect, but later was embarrassed by it, and said at one point that he never wanted to see it or hear about it again, and that no architect should be allowed to build a house before he was forty.

It is called the Red House because it is built of deep red brick, an unusual medium for a man of means, who was normally expected to build in something nobler. It rather resembles a Victorian village school in outline (or perhaps Victorian village schools resemble it!), with its steep roof and dormer windows looking like belfries; you fully expect to see a vicarage and church in the same style hovering nearby. It is the work of two young and future geniuses of their generation, who together worked out the principles of architectural truthfulness that would guide the Arts and Crafts Movement in the future.

There is a magical quality of invention about the Red House, and perhaps one's excitement is heightened by imagining Morris's friends arriving at Abbey Wood Station and driving the three miles into the country to come and stay here. Edward Burne-Jones, who had been at Oxford with Morris and then shared a London house with him, was a regular visitor. He painted scenes in an amateurish fashion from the medieval romance of Sir Degrevaunt on the lower walls of the drawing room, some of which have survived.

BRIDGE LODGE
—— Eythrope, Stone ——
BUCKINGHAMSHIRE

BRIDGE LODGE was built as an estate 'cottage', by Alice, sister to Ferdinand von Rothschild, members of the Vienna branch of this phenomenal and awe-inspiring family. By the 1880s the Rothschilds had taken the Vale of Aylesbury by storm. The Victorian worship of money was on the wax, and houses were an outward expression of what you were worth and how fashionable was your taste. Mayer Amschel Rothschild built Mentmore, Alfred Rothschild built Halton House, Lionel Rothschild rebuilt Tring, and Ferdinand built Waddesdon, all on the most spectacular scale and in the wildest styles they could muster. They employed literally thousands of Buckinghamshire men for years and years.

Ferdinand, desperate to be accepted by the *cognoscenti* and to build up political influence, flaunted his lavishness by building a gigantic French château of bright yellow Bath stone with 222 rooms, and by planting hundreds of fully grown trees on the high bare hill on which it stood. His sister Alice followed suit in a slightly less glittery way on the adjoining estate she had bought at Eythrope. Alice's estate was beautiful already with the wide shallow River Thames running through it.

The old Eythrope house which had stood near to Bridge Lodge had belonged to the Earls of Chesterfield, who had pulled it down in 1810 and made the most of the high price of building materials then prevailing owing to the Napoleonic wars. Consequently, vestiges of a great house remained in the form of mature avenues and a feeling of settled peace.

This is where the solitary and delicate Alice, whose health was her predominant worry, decided to create her little demesne. She employed the architect George Devey to build her 'Pavilion', where she would spend her days, but for fear of being made ill by the river's damp fumes she always dined and spent the night with her brother at Waddesdon. George Devey also built this sumptuously romantic Lodge for Alice, right beside a waterfall.

Devey has created a masterpiece of the Victorian Picturesque. As so many of his contemporaries did, he had a penchant for traditional cottage architecture and was particularly fond of the Kentish styles and materials, having worked for Lord de l'Isle at Penshurst. He was artistic, gentle and country loving, and though he was based in London, with an office in Great Marlborough Street, country commissions were his favourite. If your client was called Rothschild there was no such word as 'restraint'. Mr Devey went to town.

EDWARDIAN TO THIRTIES

A more stylish and dramatic return to English tradition came about through the Arts and Crafts Movement, which stood for integrity and truthfulness and believed whole-heartedly in the use of local craftsmen and materials. From those early Tudor days the English house had come full circle, but these Edwardian houses were warm, practical and comfortable; they epitomized countrified romanticism. Meanwhile, on the Continent, the modern movement was on its way to creating houses that abandoned period styles and traditional materials and forged ahead into a scientific age. They left the English house behind.

MUNSTEAD WOOD

—— Godalming ——

SURREY

THE SOPHISTICATED Miss Gertrude Jekyll, gardening heroine of the Edwardians, commissioned Edwin Lutyens to design her Surrey homestead, and this he did so beautifully that their relationship was cemented and many future joint commissions ensued. The house was built by Thomas Underwood of Dunsfold, and the stonemason was William Herbert of Whitley. The garden front, of Bargate stone, brick and tile, shows how Lutyens has exaggerated the local Surrey style to perfectly fitting proportions. The roof lines swoop, the chimneys soar, and the beams of local oak in the hall look silver with age. (This effect was achieved by spreading the timbers with hot lime for fifteen minutes and then scraping it off.) Miss Jekyll's desire (with a little help) for all that was 'thorough and honest of spirit of the good work of old days', the creed of the Arts and Crafts Movement, was fulfilled. Munstead Wood, with its half-timbered north-west side, its kitchen courtyard, its ingle-nooks and its superb craftsmanship, became a show-piece of its time.

Lutyens was brought up at Thursley in Surrey and developed a great love for that county's local styles and materials, although he also built in the grandest of manners. One of the reasons for his having such innovative ideas was that he was almost untrained, some would say untrainable, and laughed (extremely annoyingly at the time) at his elders and betters and their obsessions with sketching and learning the orders. After spending two years at the South Kensington School of Art, he went for a year to the office of the architect Sir Ernest George when he was still only eighteen.

Towards the end of his life he told Osbert Sitwell; 'Any talent I may have was due to a long illness as a boy, which afforded me time to think, and subsequent ill-health, because I was not allowed to play games, and so had to teach myself, for my enjoyment, to use my eyes instead of my feet.'

The greatest Scottish architect of his time, Sir Robert Lorimer, was enchanted when he visited Munstead Wood in 1897. He wrote to his friend R.S. Dods in Australia, '. . . it looks so reasonable, so kindly, so perfectly beautiful, that you feel that people might have been making love, and living and dying there and dear little children running about for – the last – I was going to say 1,000 years – anyway, 600. They've used old tiles which of course helps – but the proportion, the way the thing's built . . . "by the old people of the old materials in the old unhurrying way" but at the same time "sweet to all modern uses" . . . and who do you think did this for her? – a young chap called Lutyens, 27 he is – and I've always heard him derided by the Schultz school as a "society" architect. Miss J. has pretty well run him and now he's doing a roaring trade and has just married a daughter of Lord Lytton, he's evidently right in with the right lot of people . . . and what a God's mercy that for once in a way these people have got hold of the right man and what a thing for England.'

BROADLEYS

Windermere

WESTMORLAND

'OWING TO its natural beauty, protected situation and other attractive features, Windermere is popular not only as a holiday resort, but as a permanent summer and winter residence. It is entirely modern and in its environs are many residential villas embowered in trees and shrubs and surrounded by beautiful gardens,' reads a guide to the Lakes of the 1900s. Travelling south along the lake-side road, through the village of Bowness (rightly pronounced Bowness by the locals, and Boness by nearly everybody else), the scenery becomes more dramatic, the villas more sparsely spaced and hidden among the maturity of their Edwardian planting. At Gill Head, where Cartmel Fell looms huge to the south and the road is dark with overhanging trees, a hidden drive turns sharply towards the lake and suddenly one of the crown jewels of the Arts and Crafts Movement is before you.

Wordsworth had lived in and loved the Lakes for sixty years, and later Ruskin, the great architectural influence of the nineteenth century, built a house on Lake Coniston. As has often been the case, it is the artists who are the forerunners of fashion, and fifty years later the world and his wife craved for Windermere. In 1897 Mr and Mrs Currer Briggs bought the most idyllic site they could lay their hands on and wrote to Mr Voysey the architect.

By this time a new aesthetic movement was evolving. Mr and Mrs Currer Briggs longed for that combination of romance and practicality which the Arts and Crafts Movement promised. Mr Charles Annesley Voysey did not disappoint them.

The main block of Broadleys faces west towards the lake above terraced gardens designed by Mr Mawson. The service block comes off at a right angle at the back and forms a sort of court where you arrive. Here on this east side are the exaggerated sweeping gables, the cottagey front door with its hinges forged with heart-shaped ends (a trade mark of Mr Voysey), the elaborate gutters, the pebble-dash over the two-feet-thick stone walls, and the cosy, comforting scale of the whole, so nice to come home to on a wet and windy evening.

On the west side the great grey Westmorland slated roof dominates the three two-storey bay windows. The hall takes up the central bay through the two storeys; the dining- and drawing-rooms are on either side. Above these are the two main bedrooms with their spectacular views up and down the lake. It is an extremely practical house, having seven bedrooms, two bathrooms, a playroom, a kitchen and the usual domestic offices.

Voysey stood for a drastic and stylized return to English country tradition and, along with Charles Rennie Mackintosh, relied on simplicity of composition for greatest effect. Their influence was revolutionary. Voysey's interiors were almost puritanically plain and, like his hero Morris, he designed his own furniture.

FOURACRE

—— West Green ——

HAMPSHIRE

'THE PLANNING is without doubt the most important thing in the designing of a house. "To be happy at home is the ultimate result of all ambition." No one can be quite happy in an ill-planned house any more than in ill-fitting clothes, and although the "cut" and "style" are much, they count for nothing in a garment which pinches and annoys the wearer in a hundred ways . . .' So wrote the architect of Fouracre, Ernest Newton.

Tucked into cosy woodland near the silver birchy Surrey border, Fouracre (which was never a four-acre site, but started as fifty) is a supremely satisfactory house. It was built for Doctor Wills and his family, whose initials are let into the circles of brickwork in the gables. It sports twenty-two chimneys and wonderful criss-cross brick-work known as 'diaperwork'. If Doctor Wills couldn't decide whether he liked sash or casement windows, then he had a choice: sash in the reception rooms and casement everywhere else.

Ernest Newton was a quiet and restrained product of the artistic circle within which he worked. He had started in Norman Shaw's office and was much encouraged by him. In the early 1880s Newton opened his Hart Street rooms in London for meetings of the St George's Art Society, which he founded and which was designed 'for the discussion of Art and Architecture'. By 1884 it had become the Art Workers' Guild, the hub of the Arts and Crafts Movement, which aimed to bring back all the fine and craft arts and to follow the writings of Ruskin and William Morris. The nineteenth century had brought mass production in the wake of its industrial revolution, and this reversion to the home-made and hand hewn was a natural reaction. Ernest Newton, like his name, was a modest and serious architect who believed in moderation.

'Building must fall into some sort of style,' he wrote ' memory – inherited forms and ideas. But this must be accepted not sought. Pass all through the mill of your mind and don't use forms unmeaningly, like buttons on the back of a coat . . . although house building is very much a practical art the practical elements may be met gracefully and pleasantly, there is scope for dignity, humour and even romance. Our house building ought to develop naturally . . . a natural architecture is a rational healthy builder's art expressing itself soberly through the medium of masonry and carpentry.'

LINKENHOLT MANOR

—— Andover ——

HAMPSHIRE

LINKENHOLT MANOR exemplifies the best sort of modest solid Edwardian country house. Comfortable and friendly, it is a broader, homelier version of the 'Queen Anne' style, which had been conceived over thirty years earlier by the great Richard Norman Shaw, and which eventually became so settled and familiar in suburban streets throughout England. It had little to do with the real Queen Anne architecture of the early eighteenth century, but merely borrowed some of its features, such as, here at Linkenholt: the thick glazing bars on the dormer windows, the shell-shaped pediment over the central dormer, and the gently hipped roof lines. These features were then mixed up with features from the local cottages of Surrey and Sussex – the tiled roof, the tile-hung wall and the gable. The interior tells the same story, incorporating high quality panelling to Queen Anne proportions, and cottagey casement windows.

The previous fifty years had provided so many alternative and revolutionary styles, that architects and clients alike often found themselves in a quandry as to which to go for. Whereas the great architectural theorists of the day and leaders of style spun their philosophy and bossed their clients about, they built few private houses between them. Men like Pugin, Ruskin and William Morris turned a distasteful and then a blind eye to the fast growing urban sprawl and preferred to live in genuine or fake medieval houses by rivers or lakes. Their influence, however, was incalculable, and the most famous of its exponents was the prolific Richard Norman Shaw. His was a free style of architecture which embraced bits of everything, and it was he, together with his friend and partner Nesfield, who invented the 'Queen Anne' style.

For a thousand years there has been a manor on this site, which belonged to Hesdins, Wriothosleys, Badds and Worgans until the nineteenth century. Then the Colsons bought the estate and, with typical Victorian model behaviour, began to smarten up the ramshackle village of Linkenholt. They commissioned William White to build the church in 1871, built a school and new cottages, pulled down the old manor and the cottages surrounding it and erected a large Victorian house. In 1886 they ran out of money and the bank foreclosed. In 1902 the house burned down while in the ownership of Mr Charles Julius Knowles. His sons received the news by telegram and were apparently unperturbed. A few years later this latest manor house was built, and in 1928 almost the first double glazing ever seen in England was installed to combat the bitterly cold winds.

Linkenholt is the highest village in Hampshire, 700 feet up, with its estate rising to 900 feet. The first combine harvester ever used in England was in service here and, in 1935, agricultural history was made when bread was eaten from wheat harvested, dried, milled and baked in the same day.

KELLING HALL

—— Holt ——

NORFOLK

Sir Edward Maufe, the architect of Kelling Hall, died on his ninety-first birthday in 1974. He was a tall, handsome and courteous man who lived in a Surrey farmhouse with off-white walls, limed oak furniture, Eric Gill sculptures and giant-leaved zimmer lindens. His most famous building was Guildford Cathedral, which he built in 1932. Maufe's obituary read, 'His work is not likely to appeal to the present generation of architects because it was essentially traditional and restrained.'

If this was true, then what a lot they missed! Kelling Hall was Maufe's first country house, built on the daring 'Butterfly' plan, so called on account of its shape. Sometimes called 'Sun Trap' houses, the idea behind them was to catch the sun at every angle. Whereas the Victorians had an aversion to the sun, and sometimes faced new houses to the north, the well-off Edwardians worshipped it. They ventured under its rays for breakfast and tea and lolled about in it during the afternoons. The other side of Kelling has the same outward-slanting wings, shielding a terrace from which the garden slopes gently away to the wide Norfolk view.

It was Richard Norman Shaw who first conceived the idea when he was remodelling a Northumbrian house called 'Chesters'. His pupil E.S. Prior then refined and glamorized the idea and became the most celebrated and earliest 'Butterfly' specialist. He built a thatched 'Butterfly' at Exmouth for a fellow old Harrovian called Major Weatherby, and the wildly eccentric 'Home Place' just outside Holt. It was the latter which so struck Henry Detterding, the Director General of the Royal Dutch Petroleum Company, who resolved to build himself a 'Butterfly' house and commissioned Maufe.

Norfolk is a county poor in stone, particularly in the north, where flint is widely used as a building material, with brick dressings. Maufe imported Dutch brick under instruction from the Dutch Mr Detterding and set it round the flints, which were 'knapped', that is, cut to make a smooth face rather than left whole.

Roderick Gradidge, a scholar of the 'Butterfly' plan period, explains the appeal in his book *Dream Houses*: 'Firstly it seems logical, for from a central core of the hall and staircase, the wings pushed out catching the sun and view. But also, and for architects of this period more importantly, the silhouette created by the plan had the advantage of being symmetrical and romantically complex at the same time.'

INGLEWOOD

—— Ledsham ——

CHESHIRE

INGLEWOOD, BUILT for a self-made million-aire by an unknown Arts and Crafts archi-tect in the highly desirable Wirral, epitomizes the lavish taste of the Edwardian era. By the 1900s, British Arts and Crafts houses were admired all over the world. They were a step in a different direction from the exotic and thea-trical Victorian house, and they were built for a more architecturally educated and indepen-dent type of client. Wives were given a say for the first time, and what they wanted was romantic practicality. Many took the *Studio* magazine, which showed the very latest dom-estic designs.

It was not only the cottages of Surrey, Sussex and Kent that inspired the Arts and Crafts architects; there was also a strong move-ment in Cheshire, where a wealth of clients wanted new homes not too far from the great cities of Liverpool and Manchester. Most of these new rich were only one step removed from village life, and to have a brand new 'cot-tage style' house, and on an enormous scale, was for them extremely appealing. Seasoned wood, and fires that drew, and casement windows that opened and shut perfectly and admitted no draughts were all hallmarks of the Arts and Crafts architects, who liked to use local craftsmen, local materials and effect complete harmony with the surroundings.

Mr Fox had become a millionaire through his marine insurance company in Liverpool. He did not want a classical house, but some-thing cosy and as English as could be. Whereas the Victorians had gone a bit 'foreign' with some of their house designs, Inglewood was as English as you could get, and looked like a clean, clear-cut, practical version of Cheshire's most famous half-timbered house, Little Moreton Hall. Half-timbering is Cheshire's speciality, after all – what better examples in the country are there than Handforth, Hen-bury and the spectacularly lavish Hill Bark, built in 1894 (at a cost of £150,000) and moved lock, stock and barrel in 1929 to a site five miles away in order to avoid the view of encroaching development! 'No style of building,' wrote Mr Ould, Hill Bark's architect, of half-timbering, 'will harmonize so quickly and completely with its surroundings . . . and none continues to live on such terms of good fellowship with other materials, whether rosy brickwork, grey lichen covered masonry, or pearly flag-slates.' Inglewood must have been a perfect foil for the grand civic buildings of Liverpool, with its open timber balcony on the south side over-looking terraced and formal gardens laid out in the 'Old English' style.

THE GATE HOUSE
—— Limpsfield ——
SURREY

THE OLD village of Limpsfield rises southwards with views to the chalk downs in the blue half-distance. A little out of it is the Gate House, built in the local Surrey style by Hugh Baillie Scott, for a refined and progressive family who were among the new wave of Surrey homesteaders brought here by suburban railways, and hence having the possibility of commuting. These were the new country people who, like their architects, wanted to experience 'the simple life'. No hunting, shooting or fishing for them, but walking and gardening and breathing in the clear air.

Baillie Scott was the progenitor of the American open plan and the most innovative interior decorator the first few decades of the twentieth century ever saw. He came from a family of fourteen and was brought up in Ramsgate. He started his own practice in the Isle of Man and built his first house, half-timbered and tile-hung, in the town of Douglas in 1892. His schemes for interiors and furniture were stylized, exquisitely coloured in pale greens and mauves, but often too far-fetched for clients to dare to execute them. He had a large following in Germany and was a great admirer of the American 'Shingle School' of architects, notably the work of White, Mead and McKim. His beautiful watercolours of rooms were constantly given huge spreads in the *Studio* magazine, the most important Arts and Crafts periodical.

On writing about his perfect country house, Baillie Scott is adamantly opposed to the vulgar and proposes what he considers to be the simple open plan way of life: 'Having arrived at the central idea of a hall or living room as the keynote of a home it follows naturally that one must group round this the various other rooms . . . first the "ladies' bower", the "drawing-room" as we now call it. This is a recess in the hall which is set apart for tea and music and is characterized by a certain daintiness of treatment which bears a feminine relation to the masculine ruggedness of the hall . . . at the opposite end is the "refectory". . . . Here one catches a glimpse of a table bright with silver, glass, and flowers against the dark background of the seating which runs round three sides of the table . . . one must not omit to mention the obvious adaptability of the hall to festive occasions. The underlying idea of the central focus with its grouped dependencies here exactly meets the requirements of the case, and one need not hesitate as to whether the drawing-room or the dining-room carpet should be taken up for dancing . . . .'

UNDERTOWN
—— Trebetherick ——
CORNWALL

UNDERTOWN REEKS of quality; with its great organic chimney and its sumptuous flaunting of local materials, it is a last blast of true Arts and Crafts architecture. The 'village' of Trebetherick has a rarefied air; it keeps apart and does not like to mix with its brash neighbour Polzeath, whose villas are shoulder to shoulder, nor with the heartier village of Rock, where strong men sail small boats. At Trebetherick you paddle on Daymer Bay, or shrimp off Gully, or collect cowries on Greenaway. The pervading atmosphere is one of the 1910s and 1920s, and the tone is set by the holiday houses hiding, like Undertown, among macracarpa trees, or braving it on the cliff with their faces looking to the Atlantic.

The summer visitors to Trebetherick were generally the families of retired headmasters of minor public schools, of ex Indian Civil servants or of Harley Street doctors. They felt comfortable in sand shoes and bungalows. Ernest Betjemann, however, who built Undertown, was in trade; he was the son of a cabinet-maker and managed a prosperous business manufacturing inlaid cigar boxes and elaborate cocktail cabinets for Maharajas. He was rather looked down on by the Trebetherick set. At first he and his family hired a house called 'Linkside'. However, little by little, as Aspreys sold more and more of his artefacts, so Ernest bought up more and more land along the cliff and through the village. He ended by building his dream house in the cosy lee of a gentle hill and away from the roar of the sea.

Ernest had an eye for detail, and Undertown displays this to the hilt. Every wooden door latch still lifts and drops perfectly, every moulded stone in the ingle-nook is smooth as silk. The architect was Robert Atkinson, a shrewd-looking man with sharp features and reddish hair. He had designed the first 'luxury' cinemas in the land, the most famous of which was the Regent in Brighton, showing that you could be lavish without being vulgar. Ernest and he had met on the golf links and both shared a love of collecting antiques. Although Atkinson was a modernist in principle, he was also capable of building in the true Arts and Crafts tradition.

Undertown was designed as a summer holiday house, facing south towards the dunes and up the Camel Estuary, with a view across the golf links to the church of St Enodoc and Brae Hill beyond. There is a spacious loggia, and several nooks well out of the wind. In the shallow sloping terraced garden, with drystone retaining walls, there is a sunken circular garden with a seat all round it and a slate floor which was used for having tea in the shade on boiling afternoons. When Ernest's widow sold Undertown and all her land there, she left a proviso to future builders which contained a strict building code. This code, which is still adhered to, specifies that roofs must be made of slate, all woodwork must be white, and walls must be built in local stone or rendered white; it also specifies that houses must be a certain distance apart.

ASHLEY CHASE

—— Abbotsbury ——

DORSET

'At the top of Wears Hill we could just make out a signpost, pointing inland to Ashley Chase. We followed it, passed a massive Iron Age earthwork called Abbotsbury Castle, and gradually entered an isolated valley shielded from the sea by the massive bulk of Wears Hill. As we slowly descended, the mist cleared a little, and we found ourselves amid sheep pastures . . .' wrote the late Louis Littman, a successful businessman, when he and his wife first saw Ashley Chase with a view to buying it. 'The particulars we had been given referred to an estate of 680 acres having four cottages and a stone house . . . This was no shabby, run-down Victorian house as we had expected, but a splendid stone-clad manor house with golden hamstone mullions, and a greenish roof of Cornish Delabole slate. It presented a varied façade, full of gables, stone chimneys, projecting wings, and even a round tower capped with a bronze weather-vane in the form of a galleon.

'We were shown over the house. There were six bedrooms on the first floor and a further two in a small staff flat above, and from every window a different view of the adjacent hills and woods. The architect had sited the house on the slope of a hill commanding a great variety of scenery and had given each bedroom its own special view. The dining-room, drawing-room, parlour and kitchen were all of good but reasonable size.'

Sir Guy Dawber, a former president of the RIBA, built Ashley Chase, hidden in this most secret of Dorset valleys. He had worked along with Lutyens in the office of Sir Ernest George and set up a practice in Bourton on the Hill, Gloucestershire, where he was kept in constant commission by the smart hunting crowd. Sir Guy was a great and unsung country house architect, a staunch traditionalist and one who loved the Cotswold style the best. His clients were private people who did not want publicity. (Lutyens' fame had grown not least because he was a great friend of the editor of *Country Life*, and likewise Voysey knew the editor of *The Studio*.) Sir Guy had little or no publicity; he wrote books about Cotswold architecture and mixed with the arty-crafty Sapperton Set – the Gimsons, Barnsley and Norman Jewson. Ashley Chase epitomized his style. 'It was a masterpiece of harmony,' wrote Littman, 'which can be attained when men see to it that their handiwork blends with their natural surroundings. The whole valley seemed to be under a spell, in a timeless past unaffected by wars, the scars of industrial development and the trauma of social upheaval.'

Louis Littman *did* buy Ashley Chase, after that first visit in 1966, and realized his childhood dream of owning and running the ideal estate. His son continues to do so.

CHERRY HILL

—— Wentworth ——

SUNNINGDALE, BERKSHIRE

HERE ENDETH the English house in the country. Cherry Hill is in the 'International Modern' style and could equally well be on the outskirts of Stuttgart or San Francisco as Sunningdale. It was a style which heralded the beginning of the end of England's architectural identity. The new buildings in our towns and cities began to look like any other new buildings in the rest of Europe. Sometimes called the 'Jazz Modern' style, International Modern was a term coined in the United States to refer to the new architectural style of the twentieth century, which architects like Frank Lloyd Wright and Walter Gropius were creating before the First World War. Cherry Hill admirably demonstrates all the style's characteristic features – white rendering, asymmetrical cubic shapes, large windows and a complete absence of mouldings. (The recessed verandah to the right of centre, with its sliding picture windows, was added at a later date.) At the time it appalled the traditionalists; now it is winning them round with its logical elegance, nostalgic glamour and atmosphere of cocktails on a Cunard liner.

Oliver Hill, its architect, was a chameleon who could perform miracles and build in whatever style was asked of him by his upper-class clients, some of whom were startlingly 'progressive'. Whether it be in 'International Modern', Organic Arts and Crafts, Neo-Elizabethan, Neo-Jacobean, or Neo-Georgian, Hill could accommodate his client. In 1948 he moved to the ancient house of Daneway, near Sapperton, where he ground his own flour, baked his own bread and made his own paper on which to print his poems on his own press. What a far cry from the 'machine for living in' which Cherry Hill was meant to be.

The *Architect and Building News* of 10 January 1936 reported: 'Mr Oliver Hill's romantic modernism has rarely found a happier destination than this charmingly picturesque house in the woods near Virginia Water. The site, on the crest of a hill, is sheltered by a group of scotch firs and to the south an open view extends over Cobham Common. . . . All the living and bedrooms are placed on the south side, facilitating the effective area of plain wall on the north. The dining-room and sitting-room which both open into each other display rectangular wall sections of selected birch, slightly pink toned and white waxed. . . . The sitting-room has glazed sliding-front china cases, electrically lit on either side. . . the staircase window, or rather glass wall, has fringed curtains in green and white, illuminated from below at night time.'

BIBLIOGRAPHY

GENERAL

Arts Council of Great Britain, *Lutyens: The Work of the English Architect Sir Edwin Lutyens, 1869-1944* (Arts Council, 1981).

Aslet, Clive, *The Last Country Houses* (Yale University Press, 1982).

Barley, M.W., *The English Farmhouse and Cottage* (Alan Sutton, 1987).

Barrett, Helena and Phillips, John, *Suburban Style: The British Home, 1840-1960* (MacDonald Orbis, 1987).

Betjeman, Sir John, *A Pictorial History of English Architecture* (John Murray, 1972).

Brown, R.J., *English Farmhouses* (Robert Hale, 1982).

Brown, Roderick, (Ed.), *The Architectural Outsiders* (Waterstone, 1985).

Brunskill, R.W., *Illustrated Handbook of Vernacular Architecture* (Faber and Faber, 1978).

Cave, Lyndon F., *The Smaller English House* (Robert Hale, 1981).

Clifton-Taylor, Alec, *The Pattern of English Building* (Faber and Faber, 1972).

Clifton-Taylor, Alec, *Buildings of Delight* (Victor Gollancz with Peter Crawley, 1986).

Colvin, H.M., *A Biographical Dictionary of English Architecture, 1660-1840* (John Murray, 1954).

Cook, Olive and Smith, Edwin, *The English House through Seven Centuries*, (Penguin Books, 1968).

Cook, Olive and Smith, Edwin, *English Cottages and Farmhouses* (Thames and Hudson, 1954).

Darley, Gillian and Toler, Pamela, *The National Trust Book of the Farm* (The National Trust/Weidenfeld and Nicolson, 1981).

Davis, Terence, John Nash, *The Prince Regent's Architect* (Country Life, 1966).

Dixon, Roger and Muthesius, Stefan, *Victorian Architecture* (Thames and Hudson, 1978).

Downes, Kerry, *English Baroque Architecture* (A. Zwemmer, 1966).

Eberlein, Harold Donaldson, *Little Known England* (B.T. Batsford, 1930).

Fedden, Robin and Joekes, Rosemary, *The National Trust Guide* (Jonathan Cape, 1973).

Fawcett, Jane, *Seven Victorian Architects* (Thames and Hudson, 1976).

Girouard, Mark, *Life in the English Country House* (Yale University Press, 1978).

Girouard, Mark, *The Victorian Country House* (Clarendon Press, Oxford, 1971).

Gradidge, Roderick, *Dream Houses: The Edwardian Ideal* (Constable, 1980).

Gotch, J. Alfred, *The Growth of the English House* (B.T. Batsford, 1928).

Hitchcock, Henry-Russell, *Early Victorian Architecture in Britain* (The Architectural Press, 1954); *Early Victorian Architecture in Britain 2* (The Architectural Press, 1954); *Architecture: Nineteenth and Twentieth Centuries* (Pelican History of Art, Penguin Books, 1958).

Howard, Maurice, *The Early Tudor Country House* (1987).

Lutyens, Mary, *Edwin Lutyens* (John Murray, 1980).

Mercer, Eric, *English Vernacular Houses*

Mogg, Edward, *Paterson's Roads* (Langman, Hurst, Rees, Orme, and Brown, 1822).

Williams-Ellis, C. & A., *The Pleasures of Architecture* (Jonathan Cape, 1924).

Montgomery-Massingberd, Hugh, *The Field Book of Country Houses and their Owners, Family Seats of the British Isles* (Webb and Bower with Michael Joseph, 1988).

Mordaunt Crook, J., *The Greek Revival* (John Murray, 1972).

Osbaldeston, George, *Squire Osbaldeston: His Autobiography* (John Lane/The Bodley Head, 1926).

Pakington, Humphrey, *English Villages and Hamlets* (B.T. Batsford, 1934).

Pilcher, Donald, *The Regency Style* (B.T. Batsford, 1947).

Ramsey, Stanley C. and Harvey, J.D.M., *Small Georgian Houses and their Details, 1750-1820* (The Architectural Press, London, 1972).

Richardson, C.J., *The Englishman's House* (Chatto and Windus).

Richardson, Margaret, *Architects of the Arts and Crafts Movement*

Robinson, John Martin, *The Latest Country Houses* (The Bodley Head, 1984).

(Trefoil Books, 1983).

Saint, Andrew, *Richard Norman Shaw* (Yale University Press).

Service, Alastair (Ed.), *Edwardian Architecture and its Origins* (The Architectural Press, 1975).

Soane, John, *Plans, Elevations and Sections of Buildings* (Gregg, 1971); *Sketches in Architecture* (Gregg, 1971).

Stamp, Gavin, and André Goulancoust *The English House 1860-1914* (Faber 1986).

Thorne, R.G., *The Commons, 1790-1820*.

Turnor, Reginald, *The Smaller English House, 1500-1939* (B.T. Batsford, 1952).

Wenham, Valerie, *The National Trust Handbook* (The National Trust, 1988).

Whistler, Laurence, *Sir John Vanbrugh, Architect and Dramatist, 1664-1726* (Cobden-Sanderson, 1938).

Willmott, Ernest, *English House Design* (Batsford 1911).

Wilson, Derek, *Rothschild: a Story of Wealth and Power* (André Deutsch, 1988).

Wilton, The Earl of, *On the Sports and Pursuits of the English* (Harrison, 1868).

REGIONAL

Aubrey, John and Jackson, John Edward, *Wiltshire, the Topographical Collections* (Wiltshire Archaeological and Natural History Society, 1862).

Barker, H.R., *East Suffolk Illustrated* (F.G. Paisey, 1908-9); *West Suffolk* (F.G. Paisey, 1907).

Betjeman, John and Piper, John, *Murray's Berkshire Architectural Guide* (John Murray, 1949).

The Beauties of England and Wales Series, (Venar & Hood).

Cecil, David, *Some Dorset Country Houses: A Personal Selection* (Dovecote Press, 1988).

De Figueiredo, Peter and Treuherz, Julian, *Cheshire Country Houses* (Phillimore, 1988).

Delderfield, Eric R., *West Country Houses and their Families, Vol. 2: Dorset, Wiltshire and North Somerset* (David and Charles, 1970).

Elyard, S.J., *Old Wiltshire Homes* (1894).

Fleetwood-Hesketh, Peter, *Murray's Lancashire Architectural Guide* (John Murray, 1955).

Glover, *History and Gazetteer of Derbyshire* (1829).

Gurney, Samuel, *Isabel Mrs Gurney, afterwards The Lady Talbot De Malahide, 1851-1932* (Jarrold and Sons, Norwich; Simpkin Marshall, London).

Shell Guides series: (Faber and Faber).

Highways and Byways (Series, MacMillan).

Hudson, L.W.G., *Ancient Parish of Frampton: A Short History of the Church and Village.*

Lees-Milne, James, *Some Cotswold Country Houses: A Personal Selection* (Dovecote Press, 1987).

Littman, L.T.S., *Ashley Chase, a Dorset Domain* (Alan Sutton, 1988).

Palmer, Sutton and Mitton, G.E., *Buckinghamshire and Berkshire* (A. & C. Black, 1920).

Pevsner, Nikolaus, *The Buildings of England* (Series, Penguin).

Burke's and Savills Guide to Country Houses, Vols. I-III: Shute, Henry, My Lord Pembroke's Manor of Netherampton (Henry Shute, 1986).

Stanton, Phoebe, *Pugin* (Thames and Hudson, 1971).

Adam brothers, 81
Alderly Grange, Wotton Under Edge, Gloucestershire, 96
Allerthorpe Hall, Gatenby, East Riding, Yorkshire, 33
Ardington House, 89
Ashdown Park, 76
Ashley Chase, Abbotsbury, Dorset, 169
Atkinson, Robert, 167

Barnham Hall, Chichester, Sussex, 40
Barry, Sir Charles, 136, 140
Beckley Park, Beckley, Oxfordshire, 7, 17
Bedgebury, 13
Betjemann, Ernest, 167
Bettiscombe, Bridport, Dorset, 52
Biddesden House, Ludgershall, Wiltshire, 79
Biddick Hall, Lambton Park, County Durham, 85
Bodley, G.F., 142
Bridehead, Little Bredy, Dorset, 132
Bridge Lodge, Eythrope, Stone, Buckinghamshire, 149
Brizlincote Hall, Bretby, Derbyshire, 69
Broadleys, Windermere, Westmorland, 155
Browne, Robert, 59
Burlington, Lord, 43
Butterfield, 140

Came House, Dorchester, Dorset, 103
Campbell, Colin, 82
Carr, John, 110
Carter, John, 109
Cartwright, Francis, 103
Casterton Hall, 114
Chambers, Sir William, 123
Cherry Hill, Wentworth, Sunningdale, Berkshire, 170
Church Farm, Stanton Lacy, Shropshire, 104
Cockerell, 140
Compton Beauchamp, Shrivenham, Berkshire, 76
Coxe's Hall, Stanford in the Vale, 89
Croan, Wadebridge, Cornwall, 7, 56
Crow Wood, Stokesley, Yorkshire, 74

Daukes, Samuel Whitfield, 140
Dawber, Sir Guy, 169
Devey, George, 149
Dobson, John, 131
Dormington House, Dormington, Herefordshire, 106
Dunster Castle, Somerset, 28

Easby Hall, 74
Easton Neston, 124
Ebberston Hall, Ripon, Yorkshire, 82
Edwardian to Thirties architecture, 151-171

Forest House, Chigwell, Essex, 123
Forston Manor, Charminster, Dorset, 59

Fouracre, West Green, Hampshire, 156
Frampton Court, 59
Gate House, Limpsfield, Surrey, 164
George, Sir Ernest, 63, 68, 152, 169
Georgian architecture, 82-116
Gerbier, 47
Gibbs, James, 96
Gropius, Walter, 170

Hagge Farm, Nether Handley, Staveley, Derbyshire, 34
Halfpenny, John, 100
Halfpenny, William, 100
Hall, Horningham, 51
Harboard, Felix, 75
Hareston Farm, Brixton, Devonshire, 7, 10
Heligan, Mevagissey, 56
Heydon Hall, 20
Hill, Oliver, 170
Hill Bark, 163
Hinderton Hall, Neston, Cheshire, 145
Horder, Morley, 30

Iford Manor, Wiltshire, 70
Inglewood, Ledsham, Cheshire, 163

Jones, Inigo, 39, 40, 43

Kellaways, Chippenham, Wiltshire, 44
Kelling Hall, Holt, Norfolk, 160
Kew Palace, 40
Kingston House, Kingston Bagpuize, 89
Knockhill, Scotland, 6

Lake House, Frampton Court, Frampton on Severn, Gloucestershire, 100
Lambton Castle, 85
Leck Hall, Kirby Lonsdale, Lancashire, 114
Letheringsett, Holt, Norfolk, 120
Ley, The, Weobly, Herefordshire, 24
Linkenholt Manor, Andover, Hampshire, 159
Little Moreton Hall, 163
Lodge Park, Sherborne, Gloucestershire, 7, 43
Lorimer, Sir Robert, 152
Lumley Castle, 85
Lutyens, Sir Edwin, 70, 73, 152, 167
Lyndon Hall, 47

Mackintosh, Charles Rennie, 155
Manor Farm Hammoon, Sturminster Newton, Dorset, 28
Manor Farm, West Challow, Stanford in the Vale, Berkshire, 89
Manor House, Poulton, Gloucestershire, 48
Manor House, Sandford Orcas, Dorset, 14
Marlborough House, 39, 47
Maufe, Sir Edward, 160
Midford Castle, Bath, Somerset, 109
Morris, William, 73, 135, 146

Mothecombe House, Holberton, Devonshire, 6, 7, 73
Munstead Wood, Godalming, Surrey, 152
Nash, John, 119, 131
Netherhampton House, Wilton, Wiltshire, 6, 66
Newton, Ernest, 156
Newton Ferrers, 73

Old Rectory, Farnborough, Wantage, Berkshire, 99
Old Rectory, Holt, Norfolk, 86
Old Rectory, St Colomb Major, Cornwall, 142
Old Rectory, Whittington, Lancashire, 93
Oswaldkirk Hall, Ampleforth, Yorkshire, 51
Ould, 163

Palladio, Andrea, 81, 82
Papworth, John, 123
Parham Old Hall, Parham, Suffolk, 37
Pattenden Manor, Goudhurst, Kent, 13
Paxton, 140
Peto, Harold A., 65, 70
Pevsner, Nikolaus, 65, 79, 90, 132
Pomfret Lodge, Hulcote, Northamptonshire, 124
Prior, E. S., 160
Pugin, Augustus Welby Northmore, 135, 136, 140, 159

Queen's House, Greenwich, 39, 40

Red House, Bexley Heath, Kent, 146
Reddish House, Broad Chalke, Wiltshire, 61
Regency architecture, 117-134
Renaissance to Baroque architecture, 39-80
Repton, Humphrey, 119, 127
Restrop Manor, Purton, Wiltshire, 27
Robinson, P.F., 132
Ruskin, 136

St Marie's Grange, Alderbury, Salisbury, Wiltshire, 136
Sandridge, Stoke Gabriel, Devon, 119
Scott, Hugh Baillie, 164
Scott, Sir George Gilbert, 140, 142
Sedgebrook Manor, Grantham, Lincolnshire, 94
Shaw, Richard Norman, 135, 140, 156, 159, 160
Sheldonian, 47
Sherborne Park, 43
Sheringham Hall, Sheringham, Norfolk, 127
Shotesham, Norwich, Norfolk, 113
Sibton Park, Yoxford, Suffolk, 131
Sledmere Castle, Yorkshire, 110
Soane, Sir John, 113
South Luffenham Hall, Oakham, Rutland, 47, 48

Street, G.E., 140, 142, 146
Sturges, John, 47
Summerson, Sir John, 39
Sutton on the Hill Hall, Derby, Derbyshire, 128
Swangrove, Badminton, Chipping Sodbury,
    Gloucestershire, 62

Teulon, Samuel Saunders, 139
Toft Manor, Combeston, Cambridgeshire, 140
Trerice, Newquay, Cornwall, 18
Tudor to early Renaissance architecture, 9-38

Undertown, 167

Victorian architecture, 135-150
Voysey, Charles Annesley, 155, 169

Waddon Manor, Weymouth, Dorset, 55
Waterhouse, Alfred, 140, 145
Waterston Manor, Charminster, Dorset, 30
Wealden house structure, 13
Webb, John, 114
Webb, Philip, 135, 146

West Hanney Manor, 89
White, William, 142, 159
Widcombe Manor, Bath, Somerset, 90
Wilderhope Manor, Rushbury, Shropshire, 23
Wilkins, William, 131
Winston Grange, Debenham, Suffolk, 139
Wood Dalling Hall, Saxthorpe, Norfolk, 20
Worcester Lodge, 62
Wren, Sir Christopher, 39, 47
Wright, Frank Lloyd, 170
Wyatt, James, 109

ACKNOWLEDGEMENTS

I would like to thank the owners of all the houses for being
so helpful and for letting us take photographs.

Also thank you for help, advice and hospitality to Caroline Conran, Peregrine the Saint, Mrs Littman, Tony Lambton, Andrew Parker Bowles, 'The Manager', George Clive, Lady Mary Clive, Percy Higgs, Amanda Feilding, Diana Coleman, Lady Bengough, Mrs Liz Jackson, Mrs Daphne Hoskins, Christopher Gibbs, Geoffrey Van Cutsen, Michael Todhunter, Mrs Shirley Spearing, Desmond Priest, Jack Hickish, Mr Glen Simmonds, Mr Morely, John Selwyn Gummer, William and Sarah Bulwer Long, Tony Snowdon, Dr Bridget Wood, Mrs Hunwick, The bananamen, D.V. and Imogen.

Especial thanks to the following for being badgered without complaint: Hugh Montgomery Massingberd, Billa Harrod, Nigel Thimbleby, Gavin Stamp, Colin Amery, David Milnaric, Gervase Jackson-Stops, James Lees-Milne, Katie Till and John Martin Robinson.

Eternal thanks to Alastair Service for kindness, guidance and expert advice, to Francis Graham for brilliant and scholarly library research, and to Tracy Leeming for doing most of the work.

C.L.G.